The Book on the Topmost Shelf

by

David Lewis Paget

BARR BOOKS

For my wife,
Lynette
and my children,
Christopher, Susan, Morgan, Shea,
Blaise, Blake & Alison.

Other Poetry available by the author:

Pen & Ink — The Complete Works 1968-2008
Timepieces — The Narrative Poetry
At Journey's End — The Narrative Poetry, Vol. II
The Demon Horse on the Carousel — and Other Gothic Delights
Poems of Myth & Scare
The Devil on the Tree — and Other Poems of Dysfunction
Tales from the Magi
Taking Root
The Storm and the Tall Ship Pier
The Season of the Witch
Smugglers Pie
My China — Poetry in and about China

All Poems
Copyright © 2013-2014
By David Lewis Paget
ISBN - 978-0-9596876-0-6
All Rights Reserved

Foreword

This is the ninth book of all new, narrative poems I've published over the past five years. As each book contains a minimum of 60 poems, that makes for well over 540 poems written over that same period. (Almost a hundred more than that figure, in actual fact). So why do I persist?

Why does a musician play, an artist paint, a writer write? Because that's what we do, and we have no more control over that compulsion than you have over the traffic lights on the way to work. I publish them because they're there. I publish them so they won't become lost in the dross of time, be mislaid, displaced, or vanish forever in cyberspace.

Each tale within these pages has unraveled slowly from some tightly rolled secret hoard, stored safely up in the dark locker of an over-active imagination. They descended to pen and keyboard as tiny slivers of plot, character, background, lines, rhymes, imagery and shivery. I was the lucky one chosen to put all those pieces together in some comprehensible and entertaining fashion, that in some future time you, the reader, might pick up this book and read about your own foibles, dreams, schemes, and nightmares. You will meet long-lost friends in these pages, old lovers barely remembered except for the pain of partings, and perhaps darkly forgotten deeds that you had long ago hidden under the pillow of forgetfulness. Whatever you read here, I guarantee that you won't be bored.

David Lewis Paget   October 2014

Contents

Index of First Lines   179

1. The Book on the Topmost Shelf   7
2. Rocky Ground   10
3. Charlie's Room   12
4. The World Outside   15
5. Empty Words   18
6. The Pirate Brig & the Cove   20
7. The House of Dread   23
8. The Little Withering Rep.   26
9. Take Me!   29
10. Cockroach Castle   30
11. This is where Reason Stops!   32
12. A Life of Nothing Much   35
13. The Big Black Dog in the Yard   37
14. The Perennial Bachelor   41
15. The Hollow Tree   44
16. Ice!   48
17. The Actress   51
18. The Circle Line   53
19. The Prince in the Garden Shed   57
20. The Rival   60
21. The Wishing Well   62
22. The Devil's Drop Inn   66
23. Lost!   69
24. The Sin Eater   70
25. The End of Faery   73
26. Crow!   75
27. Next Time Around   78
28. Key to the Door   81
29. Topsy Turvy   84
30. The Yellow Doll   88

31. Shooting Star	92
32. Black & White	94
33. The Living Dead	96
34. Strange Encounter	98
35. The Last Druid	100
36. The Raggedy Man	103
37. Lobster Reef	107
38. The End of Motherly Love	111
39. The Whispering Wall	114
40. The Last Friend	116
41. Bats in the Belfry	118
42. You Can't Come In!	121
43. Drama Queen	123
44. The Village that Wasn't There!	125
45. The Face in the Passing Train	129
46. The Tide is Coming In	131
47. The Homecoming	133
48. A Long, Long Walk by the Lake	136
49. Stranger on the Beach	139
50. Frosty Hollow	141
51. The Fifty Dollar Ride	143
52. Bed of Roses	146
53. Return to the Light that Failed	149
54. Lightning Strike	152
55. The Spyders	155
56. The Storyteller	158
57. Angel Dust	160
58. The Bull Roarer	162
59. Blood, Red Blood…	165
60. Martha's Broom	167
61. Crossword	170
62. Cliffhanger	172
63. The Butcher's Hook	175

The Book on the Topmost Shelf

My uncle lived in a big old house
At the end of Mayfair Drive,
With thirteen rooms and a library,
Whilst he was still alive.
But he jumped one day from the second floor
And he hit the ground so hard
That his blood spread out like a pair of horns,
There in his own front yard.

We didn't know why he had to jump,
It wasn't a lack of cash,
His health was good, but before he jumped
He'd broken out in a rash,
The maid had brought him his morning tea
Had watched him put back a book,
Up on the topmost shelf it went
And he'd said to her, 'Don't look!'

The rash spread quickly under his arms
With pustules down in the groin,
The doctor said at the autopsy
That one was shaped like a coin.
'You'd swear that there was a devil's head
Imprinted there in his blood,
I've never seen anything like it since
And I hope that I never should.'

But my father moved us into the house
Now, with his brother gone,
He locked us out of the library
But went in there on his own.

There were shelves and shelves of books in there
And one on the topmost shelf,
The maid had whispered, 'You'd best beware!'
But he took it down himself.

I noticed he wore his patent gloves
Whenever he went in there,
I peeped in through a crack in the door
And saw him stand on a chair,
The book was old, had a mouldy look
For the leather was turning green,
It looked like a fungus, taken root,
And the whole thing looked unclean.

As days went by I began to hear
Some babble behind the door,
And incense came in a steady stream
Out from a crack by the floor,
My father didn't come out for meals
His voice was becoming hoarse,
He'd take a tray at about midday
But never a second course.

The maid resigned on the first of June
She said that she saw his face,
Was shivering uncontrollably
And muttering, 'Loss of grace!'
The cook took both of us under her wing
And swore that she'd see us fed,
But wouldn't come out of her tiny room
At dusk, she'd 'rather be dead!'

The fire broke out in the library
On a Sunday, after Mass,

I caught a glimpse of my father then,
His face was as green as grass,
The shelves and the books had grown a mould
And it spread all over the floor,
I knew I had to get out of there
And ran right out of the door.

My father leapt from the window then
Came crashing down in the drive,
I knew before I got close to him
He couldn't have been alive.
Two horns spread out from the place his head
Had crumpled into the ground,
But these were horns of a green fungi
Like the book on the shelf he'd found.

They quarantined us around that house
And came with chemical sprays,
'This fungus seems to be hard to kill,
It's going to take us days!'
They checked the wreck of the library,
I even went in myself,
With everything burnt to a crisp, still lay
A book on the topmost shelf!

Rocky Ground

The ground had rumbled for quite some time
It was only a minor quake,
The people grumbled, it came and went
But it kept them all awake,
'They say there was a volcano here
A billion years ago,
But it's long since dead, the geologists said,
And there'll be no lava flow.'

They'd built the suburb on rising ground,
And roads, right up to the peak,
The ground was rocky and unforgiving
The soil was grey and weak,
So little grew on that rising crest
Just the odd saltbush or so,
They couldn't drill through the rock beneath
To help their bushes grow.

I'd venture out and would take the air
When the house cooled down at night,
But always felt there was something there
That would make me feel uptight,
I felt the rumble, under my feet
It was like a muffled roar,
And I thought a whimsical thought one night,
It was like an old man's snore.

One night I wandered up to the crest
And I saw two bushes move,
They seemed to tremble and flutter there
Just above a ball shaped groove,

The rumble stopped as I stood and watched
From under the starlit skies,
The bushes opened to crystal orbs,
Just like a pair of eyes.

They fixed me there in their crystal stare
And I didn't dare to breathe,
The summit started to shake and move,
And then it began to heave,
The houses built on the crest fell down
It was like a huge hiccup,
And I fell tumbling to the ground
As the Mountain God stood up!

Charlie's Room

It was just on the stroke of midnight,
I was going to go to bed,
But I had to pass by Charlie's room
So I hung back there, instead,
I could hear the rattle of drums that came
From under his bedroom door,
And then the sound of a French 'Huzzah!'
From a Napoleonic war.

I thought, 'He's at it again, he's got
The Frenchies marching east,
He's going to Borodino, where
He's got a chance, at least,
He's leading the French Grand Armée
As Napoleon did before,
But I couldn't get in to stop him, as
He'd locked his bedroom door.

I shook my head and I went to bed,
There was no point hanging round,
For Charlie, he'd be up all night
'Til the Armée went to ground,
By dawn he'd have them dragging back
From the Russian ice and snow,
And wouldn't be fit to go to school
'Til he'd had a sleep, you know.

He wasn't a kid like other kids
He wouldn't play with a phone,
He didn't get into computer games
But he spent his time alone.

He didn't make friends so easily
For he never went out to play,
But stuck his head in a history book
And would read and read all day.

They said he must have been gifted in
Some strange, abnormal way,
He used his imagination for
The games he wanted to play,
His mind reached back to another time
Where the personae were dead,
And brought them back for a second chance
On the counterpane of his bed.

I caught a glimpse of the action once
In a crack through his bedroom door,
A galleon moored in a harbour by
An armed Conquistador,
He saw me there and he slammed the door
And he said, 'Don't interfere!
I'm trying to raise the English Fleet
And I can't if you're standing there!'

His mother took him to town one day
To see a psychologist,
Who said, 'He lives in a world of his own,
I think he's really blessed.
We all grow out of our childish ways
And I think he'll be the same.'
He thought it was all in Charlie's head
'Til the day that 'Little Boy' came.

He'd read and read of the second war
For a month until that day,

When I heard the aircraft engines I
Just knew, the 'Enola Gay',
I beat and beat upon Charlie's door,
Broke out in a cold, cold sweat,
But the plane took off, and I grabbed the wife
And we'd still be running yet.

We were out in the road when the roof blew off
With a mighty blast and roar,
And the mushroom cloud was curling up
While we lay, flat out on the floor,
Charlie had gone from our lives for good
With his gift, and his bag of tricks,
Hard to believe that he had the power,
For Charlie was only six!

The World Outside

It looked all right through the windows of
Our cosy sitting room,
The day was light and the sun was bright
But the house was like a tomb,
The other rooms were as cold as hell
With their stalactites of ice,
That dripped from the bedroom ceiling down
To meet the stalagmites.

I'd settled Eve on the couch and spread
A blanket round her arms,
I didn't think I should tell her, just
In case she became alarmed,
She'd spent a week in the sitting room
For she wasn't feeling well,
How do you say, 'We've fallen into
The Seventh Circle of Hell!'

They taught us the laws of physics were
Impossible to change,
Gravity, mass, and basic math
Had a certain, definite range,
But men of science had interfered
With the particle known as 'God',
They'd built the Hadron Collider and
The results, they said, were odd.

I could have told them how odd they were
When I went outside to see,
My car was covered in mushrooms
And a train sat up in the tree.

A whale was floating beneath the Moon
And a porpoise lay in the park,
The light was bright in the sitting room
But outside, it was dark.

Nothing remained the way it was
For all the colours had changed,
The lawn, the colour of strawberry jam
And the sky was rearranged,
The stars were falling like sequins in
A cluster of drops like rain,
And ice was forming up on the eaves
That tasted like champagne.

I went inside and I slammed the door,
I turned on the News at 6,
They said there'd been an apology
But it wouldn't be hard to fix,
They'd run the Collider backwards to
The way that they'd done before,
And hopefully, the 'particle God'
Would be as he'd been once more.

I sat with Eve as the sun went down
And I tried to keep her still,
Away from the hallway mirror so
She wouldn't scream or squeal,
The lines were deepening on her face
As our lease on life had lapsed,
I hoped she wouldn't go out today
With the world outside, collapsed.

The sun rose up in the morning as
It had for a million years,

And everything was familiar,
They'd run the thing in reverse.
The News went back to the good old things
We were used to, from before,
Stabbings, murders, infanticide
And that good old standby, war!

Empty Words

There are some who consider suicide,
You can see it in their eyes,
They forget the hurt of their loved ones
When they fail to say goodbyes,
They see no point in the gift of life,
Say it doesn't work for them,
But we walk on by, and we let them die
By some careless theorem.

I noticed the girl in the local church
She was down upon her knees,
Her shoulders shaking with silent sobs
As she stared at the altarpiece,
Her eyes were glazed as she walked on by
It was then that I knew, for sure,
She'd be walking off to an awful fate
If she walked alone through the door.

I caught her up and I walked with her
And I said, 'I know what you think,
But this will pass, it's a half full glass,
What you have to do is drink.'
She turned a tear-stained eye to me
And she said, 'But what would you know?
Your life is a bed of roses now,
But mine is a horror show!'

I tried to draw her out from herself
And she seemed to want to talk,
We wandered down to the Esplanade
And went for a long, slow walk,

Her parents, they were divorced, she said,
Her father had disappeared,
Her mother was mired in drugs and drink,
It was DNA she feared.

'I don't want to end like her,' she said,
'I don't want to go like him,
My older brother just hanged himself,
I don't want to go like Tim.
There's pain and heartache each way I turn,
I shouldn't be here at all,'
I put my arm round her shoulders then,
And leant on the old seawall.

'The life you have is a gift from God,
You can't just throw it away,
We all have the choice to soldier on
To a brighter, better day.'
I thought that my words had helped her then
When I left her, shaking her head,
That was at three in the afternoon,
By six o'clock, she was dead!

The Pirate Brig & the Cove

I was part of the crew of a Sloop-of-War
That had sailed in the Caribbean,
We were caught asleep in the port one night
By the crew of a Brigantine.
They loosed a broadside, seven guns
As the Skull and the Bones flew high,
And I was dragged to the pirate ship
Where they said, 'You'll serve, or die!'

There wasn't a choice to be had back then,
So I climbed aloft on the mast,
Setting the rig of the fore topsail
And making the halyards fast,
They made me stay in the Crows Nest then
To be swept by the wind and rain,
With only a couple of tots of rum
To deal with my aches, and pain.

I kept lookout on the pirate brig
For His Majesty's ships, and land,
They knew we wouldn't stand much of a chance
As a Privateer Brigand,
We sought to shelter within a cove
In an island, not on a chart,
And rowed ashore in a longboat there
With the bosun, Jacob Harte.

Captain Keague had stayed on the ship
With the bloodiest of his crew,
The rest of us had been pressed to sea
To do what we had to do.

We filled our barrels with water from
A rill that flowed from the hill,
And gathered fruit that we'd never seen
From trees with an earthy feel.

The trees had tendrils that waved about,
And trunks that were black and charred,
Just like a fire had raged there once
And left them, battle-scarred.
A voice rang out in a clearing there,
'Hey mates, head back to the sea,
Don't let the tendrils fasten on you
Or you'll all end up like me.'

And deep in the trunk was a human face
With its skin all burnt and black,
The pain was etched on his weathered skin,
'Look out, these trees attack!
We tried to burn them away, but they
Caught every one of the crew,
That fruit you carry is poison, mates,
They'll be the end of you!'

The tendrils whipped and the tendrils slashed
And they wrapped round Jacob Harte,
He hadn't much time to scream before
They seemed to tear him apart,
And each of the crew was tangled there,
Was absorbed into a tree,
I made it back to the beach that day
Though I'm anything but free.

The roots of the trees had reached on out
To the Brigantine in the bay,

Curled like manacles round its decks
And torn its masts away,
They dragged it up on the sandy beach
And they crushed it to a shell,
Caught the crew in their tendrils too
And Captain Keague as well.

I'll put this note in a bottle, send it
Floating off in the sea,
Hoping that someone picks it up,
It's the last you'll hear from me.
Don't let them seed in the world out there
These tendril trees are cursed,
And keep this Island from off the map,
If not, I fear the worst!

The House of Dread

The house had an evil aspect as
It hung out over the street,
Casting a permanent shadow there
Where the market stalls would meet,
The first floor was half-timbered, with
The ground floor made of stone,
The windows were made of pebble glass
And the window frames of bone.

No one had lived in the house for years
Til the Robinson's moved in,
A couple, straight from the wedding church
Where they'd cleansed themselves from sin,
They'd listened to all of the rumours that
The house had its share of ghosts,
But the cheapness of the peppercorn rent
Had influenced them most.

The house was built where a charnel house
Had stood in the days of plague,
Where later a debtors' prison stood
Though its history was vague,
They said there had been a gallows there
With a trapdoor through the floor,
And the arm of the ancient gallows now
Was the lintel of a door.

But the Robinson's had sailed right in
With a mop and a whisking broom,
'In no time, it'll be spic and span,'
Said Sally, within the gloom,

While Brad had opened the shutters then
To let all the light stream in,
'We'll flush the ghosts from their waiting posts
With a broom and a pound of Vim!'

They dusted down the old furniture
Left sitting since George the Fourth,
And turned the old oak table round
So the end was facing north,
'But still there's a dampness in the air,
And a tension that feels grim,'
Sally said, as they lay in bed,
And she clung, so close to him.

'Are you sure that they can't get in,' she said
'Now we've flushed them out in the street?'
But Brad was trying to understand
Why the bed was cold at his feet.
'Why are the sheets so damp,' he said,
'And they're cold, as cold as sin,'
Sally was shivering, fit to burst
Though the sun came streaming in.

They sat at the old oak table with
Their bowls of soup, home-made,
And Sally reached out to hold his hand
But he started back, dismayed,
The soup was thick in the serving bowl
It was still three-quarters full,
When a swirl in the murky liquid then
Revealed a grinning skull.

Sally shrieked, but she couldn't speak
And Brad had held his breath,

'We've got to get out of this house today,
We're surrounded here by death.'
The shutters slammed on the windows and
The doors flew shut on their own,
And barring the pebble windows were
The frames that were made of bone.

The people out in the market heard
The screams at an early hour,
Looked knowingly at each other, said,
'They have them in their power!'
And Brad was hung from the lintel when
They finally broke inside,
While Sally was dead by a grinning skull
In the dress of a new-wed bride.

The Little Withering Rep.

The Little Withering Rep. had met
To rehearse their pantomime,
They'd left it a little late for Christmas,
Could it be done in time?
'We have a choice, we can do Snow White,
Or Peter Pan would be good,
But we have the sets for another play,
'The Wicked Witch of the Wood!'

Their hands went up for 'The Wicked Witch,'
They thought it would be the best,
For Meryl Rose had a wart on her nose
And another one on her chest.
'Meryl can play the wicked witch
As I think it's understood!'
But Meryl pouted, she wanted to play
Little Red Riding Hood.

'I'm always cast as the ugly bitch,'
She cried, 'But what about her?
She always gets the plummiest parts,
The ones with a bit of flair.'
But Helen stuck her nose in the air
And sniffed, 'I'm younger than you.
You get to play the character parts,
I'm sweet, and innocent too.'

'Now let's not fight, it's a Gala Night,'
The Director said, 'Let's cast!
Norman, you'll be the noble prince,
And Fred can be Gormenghast.

Julia, you can be the Page
But you'll have to improvise,
We'll have you girt with the shortest skirt
For you have the longest thighs.'

'We'll have to steal from the other tales
For the script is not yet writ,
Helen, you get the sleeping part
For the apple that you've bit,
The littlest ones can play the dwarves
And run around on their knees,
Don't worry, Matt, you can play a bat
And hang from one of the trees.'

They all got into their costumes,
Fancy cloaks with a funny hat,
But Albert Hook had been overlooked,
He dressed as a giant rat.
'We'll write in a part for everyone,'
For some had been looking glum,
'You can be Jack and the Beanstalk, Mac,
And Tim can be 'Fi-Fo-Fum!'

The curtain raised on the opening night
To reveal a darkened wood,
A giant bat fell out of a tree
To land where the Page was stood,
She shrieked, and clung to the wicked witch
Who was straddling broom and stick,
It knocked the apple out of her hand
That rolled in the orchestra pit.

'Please can I have my apple back?'
She whispered over the lights,

The cellist was shaking his head at that,
He'd already taken a bite!
The sleeping beauty was not asleep,
The dwarves were looking dumb,
And Jack had shaken the beanstalk then
To the sound, 'Fee-Fi-Fo-Fum!'

Nobody seemed to know what to do
The rat ran over the floor,
The cellist in the orchestra pit
Then flung back the apple core,
The Witch ran over to Helen then
Who screamed in a long, high note,
'You're mad if you think I'm eating that!'
But the Witch rammed it down her throat.

After they'd called the ambulance
And carted Helen away,
The police came in for the errant Witch
And said, 'You will have to pay!
A joke's a joke, but you tried to choke
The lead with an apple core!'
While the dwarves were rolling around in fits
As the audience fled for the door.

Take Me!

She wandered down to the rocky beach
On the first Monday in June,
She wore a shawl, and carried a wreath
And sat for the afternoon,
She'd wait til the sun was sinking low
And shadows moved in the caves,
Then stride out into the rising tide
And cast her wreath on the waves.

She didn't flinch if the waves were high
Or the storm clouds brought her rain,
She gazed out past the horizon while
Her face was creased with pain,
When lightning flickered across the sky
She knew that the gods could see,
And wrung her hands with a terrible cry,
'Will none of you pity me?'

'Take me,' she cried at the rising tide,
'Take me,' she groaned at the sky,
'You've taken the only thing I loved
And not even told me why!'
She threw herself at the foam-fleck'd waves
Where the swell would rise and breach,
But ever the tide in its forward ride
Would cast her back on the beach.

She sheltered then in the echoing caves
That dotted the cliff face shore,
And tears had streamed from a source of grace
The gods had preserved once more,

She heard the echoes as waters lapped,
Or thundered in at the cave,
A voice that ever had held her rapt,
'Be brave, my love, be brave!'

She shut her eyes and she reached on out
For the source of the voice's charms,
And moaned for a distant memory
That had held her once in his arms,
But the sea was keeping his secrets now,
She could only guess, and pine,
She couldn't know that he lay below
Near the coast of Palestine.

A stranger came on the woman there,
One of the gypsy folk,
Just as the lightning flickered once
And he wrapped her in his cloak.
He took her up to the top of the cliff
Where the unknown future lies,
As she turned aside to wave goodbye
There was lovelight in his eyes.

Cockroach Castle

There's a scurrying sound of something, burrowing,
Down in the depths of the dungeons, hurrying,
Skittering, pittering-pattering, scattering
When there's a footstep, hear them chattering:
'Here come the lords, and here comes the vassal,
Tripping their way through Cockroach Castle.'

Here come the ladies, all in their finery
Tripping and sipping the wine from the winery,
Trailing their silks, their satins and bustling,
Up in the ballroom, while the rustling
Army beneath the sounds of their razzle
Is down in the depths of Cockroach Castle.

Spilling their millions up in the glooming
Out from the flagstones, terror is looming,
Up on the awnings, hung from the ceiling
Under the swish of the skirts they're stealing,
Dropping in hair, and burrowing faster,
Cockroach Castle is set for disaster.

Suddenly all of the room is screaming
Flapping of hands, the roaches are teeming,
Myriad hordes in the Carbonara,
Candles are tipped from the candelabra,
Choking smoke from the candles guttered,
Flames leap up from the ones that stuttered.

Clothing and flags and the awnings razing
Silks and satins flare up, and blazing,
Roaches in eyes and ears, they're rasping
Clogging their throats, to leave them gasping,
There isn't a lady or lord, or vassal
To come out alive from Cockroach Castle!

This is Where Reason Stops!

Giselle went down to the Supermart
For milk, and a loaf of bread,
'Don't be too long,' said her husband, Tom,
'It looks like rain ahead.'
The sky was dark and the clouds were grey
And a breeze was gusting the trees,
As she walked a block to the corner shop
The road was covered in leaves.

She tarried a while at the Mercers,
Checked the price on a bolt of silk,
Picked up a colourful tie-dyed scarf
Before collecting the milk.
She noticed the aisles were empty when
She got around to the bread,
The only girl at the checkout said:
'It looks like a storm ahead.'

The thunder came rumbling over the shop
And the rain began to pour,
Giselle had nothing to keep her dry
So stood by the sliding door,
She read the messages on the board
For Sale, to give or swaps,
But one stood out like a weeping sore,
'This is where reason stops!'

'This is where reason stops,' it said
In an ugly, spidery scrawl,
The damp had made the lettering run
And the ink dripped down the wall.

Guiselle had shivered and stepped aside
As she noticed the second line,
'You'll never be able to find your way
When caught in the tangle of time.'

The lightning flashed and it lit the store
But nobody else was there,
Not even the only checkout girl,
She'd gone, but heaven knew where.
Giselle dashed out to a clearing sky
Where the rain had ceased to pour,
She checked the time, was surprised to find
She'd been gone, two hours or more.

Tom would be more than mad, she thought
As she hurried along the way,
She'd never been able to keep good time,
For it seemed to slip away.
She never had kept her appointments
And Tom had been known to yell:
'You'd keep the Devil himself in thrall
If you went to Hell, Giselle!'

The sun was dipping beneath the earth
And leaving a twilight glow,
She noticed that all the leaves had gone
That were there, a while ago,
There were fences now she'd never seen
And some gardens overgrown,
And on the block where her house had been
She was stood there, all alone.

There wasn't a house, there wasn't a brick,
Just bushes and bundles of weeds,

And trees, she turned for a second look,
She'd planted them all from seeds.
She thought that she must have lost her way
And ran to the corner to check,
The sign, as always, said 'Shepherds Lane'
And a chill ran down from her neck.

She knocked on the screen of the house next door
And her neighbour, Ted, came out,
He cried, 'Good God! You must be a ghost,'
And called his wife with a shout.
'Where is my husband Tom,' she said,
'And where is my lovely home?'
'Your Tom's been dead for a dozen years
Since you left him here on his own!'

'The house burnt down and they cleared the block
When they found him dead inside,
It was just a year since you took off
And he said that his heart had died.'
'But I've only been two hours,' she said,
'I've just come back from the shops;
I should have known there was something wrong,
This is where reason stops!'

A Life of Nothing Much

He came on home to an empty house
In the early morning chill,
The one he'd left when his blood was up
And he'd bent her to his will.
Harsh words had passed at the very last
When he stormed on out the door,
But now the silence seemed so vast
That his heart dropped to the floor.

There wasn't a light in the passageway,
There wasn't a light on the stair,
He crept on up to the bedroom
Only to find she wasn't there.
Her clothes were gone from the cabinet,
Her shoes were not by the bed,
He sat hard down on the mattress
Next to the note she'd left, that said:

'I knew that it had to come to this,
And you must have known it too,
This marriage has never brought us bliss
As marriages ought to do,
I tried to be a devoted wife
To support your dreams, and such,
But all it brought was despair and strife
And a life of nothing much.'

A tear rolled suddenly down his cheek
And he brushed it quickly away,
He didn't want to be seen as weak
When he ventured out in the day,

Her words had cut to the very quick
For he knew she'd spoken the truth,
A wave of misery made him sick
As he softly cried, 'Oh, Ruth!'

This wasn't the way he'd planned his life,
This wasn't the way at all,
He'd met her under the coloured lights
In the barn of a country ball,
The moment he'd looked into those eyes,
And smelt the scent of her hair,
He'd whirled her into another life,
One that she said she'd share.

But none of his dreams had come to pass,
His heart and his mind were spent,
He cursed himself in the looking glass
And struggled to pay the rent.
His heart grew bitter as time went on
And he took it out on her,
And she had wept as her husband slept,
It seemed to be so unfair.

He went downstairs to the bureau,
Raised the lid, and picked up a pen,
He wanted to write some final words
To the love that he had, back when:
'Just know that I've always loved you, Ruth,
Though I'm bitter, and out of touch,
I know that I failed, and that's the truth
In a life of nothing much.'

The Big Black Dog in the Yard

They'd gone to live in an old stone house
On the further side of a hill,
'You'll come to enjoy the countryside.'
She said, 'I never will!
I'll miss my friends and the city streets,
And where will I go to shop?'
'You shop too much as it is,' he said,
'Perhaps it's the time to stop.'

He'd taken a job on a local farm,
He wanted to get away,
Away from her supercilious friends,
The ones that had made her stray.
He'd caught her necking with Edward Jones
At the Carlton, out for a drink,
The booze was seeping into her bones,
She needed to stop, and think.

She said it was only harmless fun,
He didn't mean much to her,
'He's just a friend that I've known since when,
It was just a peck, I swear.'
'Your friend's been after your skirt too long,
He drinks you into a fog,
He'll take advantage, so you beware,
I've heard that he's called 'Black Dog!'

She wandered around the house alone
When he went to work at the farm,
Scoured the house for a bottle of gin,
Or something to keep her warm.

She looked out over the countryside,
Was suddenly on her guard,
For bounding over the garden stile
Was a big black dog in the yard.

His coat was sleek, and his body lean
And his tongue lolled out of his jaw,
She took a slug of the Gilbey's Gin
Found hidden behind a door.
The dog lay panting, and stared at her
With its eyes of grim intent,
While she stared back through the window pane,
And trembled until it went.

A week went by, and it came each day,
And stared at her from the yard,
She couldn't move while the dog was there
But she kept the windows barred.
When Ben came home from his daily toil
He could see she was most upset,
'You're pale and shivering, Gail,' he said,
'What seems to be wrong, my pet?'

'I can't go into the garden, Ben,
I'm stuck in this house all day,
It's cold and lonely within these walls
Each time that you go away.'
'You need to open the doors,' he said,
'And open the windows too,
You should be letting the sun shine in
With the fresh air blowing through.'

She didn't tell him about the dog,
She thought that he'd think her mad,

'It's only a dog,' she thought he'd say,
And suddenly felt quite sad.
'I'll try,' she muttered, but shook inside
At the thought of an open door,
With a big black dog come wandering in,
And slavering at the jaw.

It came each day for another week
Then she threw the window wide,
The breeze rushed in and it calmed her down
With the scent of the countryside.
The dog came up to the window then
And it placed its paws on the sill,
Its eyes had gleamed, turned red it seemed
And it almost broke her will.

She seemed to hear in her inner ear
What the dog, in its gruff, low tones,
Was beaming into her mind, so clear,
'Come back to Edward Jones!
He'll keep you clear of the countryside
And you'll have your friends as well,'
But reflected back from the black dog's eyes
Was a scene from the depths of Hell!

That night, she spoke of the dog to Ben,
But he laughed, and shrugged it away,
'It's probably just a farmer's dog
That comes over here to play.'
'It's more than that, I'm afraid of it,
For its eyes are cruel and hard,'
Then Ben leaned over the window-sill,
The black dog stood in the yard.

It stayed a moment and then was gone,
It leapt back over the stile,
Then disappeared in a darkened field
While Ben just stood for a while.
His face was pale when he turned to Gail
And he said, 'I'll buy a gun.
He won't come worrying you again,
By God, I'll make him run!'

He came back home the following day
To a house, so cold and still,
He placed the gun on the table, then
Looked over the window-sill.
The black dog stared, and its eyes were red
As it sneered its disregard,
For a bitch went following on behind
As they both took off from the yard.

The Perennial Bachelor

My first wife went with a guy called Bob,
The carpet cleaning guy,
The second left with a man called Rob,
She said I was far too shy,
The third, an exotic dancer, I
Had met dancing round a pole,
And she took off with a guy called Sly
With a band called 'Rock 'n Roll.'

I never seemed able to keep them
Once I'd signed on the dotted line,
For everything in my bank account
Would suddenly be, 'That's mine!'
They'd take the house and they'd take the car
And they'd take my only suit,
The one that I had married them in,
(I've never been that astute!).

So I swore off women and wedding bells,
And lived in a boarding house,
I thought I'd keep myself to myself,
Was quiet as any mouse,
The landlady was a tall ash-blonde
Who would prowl outside my door,
At ten each night she would want to fight,
'Come wrestle me on the floor!'

She'd married a German Wrestler,
Whose name was 'Attack-Me Karl',
He'd watch for tenants, flirting his wife,
And then you would hear him snarl,

So I'd keep the lock on my door up-tight
When his wife tapped on my door,
'I'm not going to let you in tonight
While Attack-Me Karl's abroad!'

I met Elaine in the common room
Where she made me toast and tea,
She'd wait 'til it was quiet as a tomb,
Come over and sit by me,
She said that I fascinated her,
For I'd not even made a pass,
And Sundays, she would follow me out
Sprawl next to me on the grass.

She told me she was free as a bird,
Was anyone's there to choose,
She'd drop her top while sunning herself
While I stayed lost in my muse.
She said divorce was a terrible thing
That marriage was sanctified,
I told her I'd not marry again
And she lay on the grass, and cried.

I moved to live in a river flat
And she moved right in with me,
I said, 'You come and go as you please,'
And gave her a duplicate key.
We've lived together for twenty years
And she's never looked at a man,
But marriage has never been on the cards,
It's not been part of the plan.

She stays because she can walk away,
She stays because she is free,

She says she'd love to be married again,
While I say, 'Not to me!'
I think that women are too perverse
To be held to an altar vow,
She has no genuine hold on me
Though I love her, even now!'

The Hollow Tree

There wasn't much left of the woods out there
By the time that they built the town,
Only a dozen square miles or so
For the rest had been cut down,
They'd fenced it off for a sanctuary
For animals large and small,
So nobody knew the hollow tree,
They hadn't been there at all.

But I would go, and I'd climb the fence
When nobody was around,
And run right into the undergrowth
To feel my feet on the ground,
I'd disappear within the trees
Just yards from the boundary fence,
The leaves were thick on the path I'd pick
Where the trees were not so dense.

The woods were a magical fairyland
Where the sun speckled through the leaves,
It painted patterns of light and sound
When the treetops waved in the breeze,
And rabbits scurried across my path
As birds would twitter above,
Warning the deer of an ancient fear
That man never showed them love.

But I was sped on the wings of life
Away from the brooding eaves,
Away from the factories of strife
On a carpet of Autumn leaves,

I must have travelled a mile and a half
When I lifted my eyes to see,
The central bole of a Red Gum hole,
In the heart of an ancient tree.

It must have been twenty feet across
And more than a hundred round,
It ruled the place in a state of grace
Stood proudly on hallowed ground,
I caught my breath at its majesty
And approached the tree in awe,
Then slowly entered the hollow trunk
Through an archway, set like a door.

My eyes grew used to the gloom in there
When a voice said, 'Don't you knock?'
And there was a girl in the corner sat
In a plain and simple frock.
Her hair was fair and was tied right back
And her cheek was pale to see,
Her needle poised on a piece of quilt
With some strange embroidery.

I stood and stared in a state of shock,
Unable to breathe a word,
For standing guard on her shoulder was
A black and stately bird,
It cocked its head and it looked at me
With a bright, unblinking eye,
'Are you the one who will set me free?'
She asked, in a drawn out sigh.

The bird had opened its beak just then
And let out an evil caw,

It sat there in a threatening stance
As I backed away to the door.
'How do I set you free,' I said
'I didn't know you were here!'
'I've been enslaved in this awful cave
For the best part of a year.'

'I have to finish the magic quilt
And there's just one thread to go,
They sentenced me for my sense of guilt
And the sapphire ring I stole.
I threw the ring in the crystal stream
That babbles over the ground,
The bird is waiting the ring's return
And won't leave 'til it's found.'

The stream was merely a chain away
With a shallow, rocky bed.
I went there, skimming the surface where
It lay, the girl had said,
I saw a glitter among the stones
Reached down, and plucked the ring,
Then made my way to the hollow tree
Where I heard her, muttering.

The bird flew off from her shoulder, and
It snatched the ring from me,
Gripped it tight in its blue-black beak
And it flew from tree to tree.
I turned my eyes to the place she'd been
But the walls and the floor were bare,
There wasn't a sign of the magic quilt
And the girl, she wasn't there.

The woods are a magical fairyland
Where the sun speckles through the leaves,
And paints its patterns of light and sound
When the treetops wave in the breeze,
Where nature casts a spell on the mind
Of the one who dares, like me,
To scale the fence, and seek to find
The bole of the hollow tree.

Ice!

She'd walk on out to the balcony
Each day that it didn't hail,
Braving the bitterly cutting winds
In the search for a distant sail,
I'd wait 'til she was shivering cold
And her lips were turning blue,
Then drag her in through the open door;
Well, what was I meant to do?

She'd cry, of course, as I thawed her out
By the small, pot belly stove,
The only thing that kept us alive
In that tiny, ice-bound cove,
I'd wrap a blanket around the form
That I'd loved since I was three,
While she looked out for the love she'd lost
And I'll swear, it wasn't me!

He'd gone away on a masted barque
With the winter coming in,
Had kissed her once as he went aboard
And swore he'd be back again,
He waved just once, then he turned his back
As the barque had sailed away,
Hauling on the top gallants as
It headed out from the bay.

The three of us had been bosom friends
Until Charles had gone to sea,
But only then had professed his love
For the love of my life, Marie,

I'd been too timid to state my love,
She saw me just as a friend,
I felt that my heart was broken, when
She turned to him in the end.

But I lived up on the cliff-top face
With a perfect view of the bay,
I'd see him first when he sailed back home
So she asked if she could stay,
She settled in, and my heart had grieved
As I watched her pale blue eyes,
Skimming the far horizon as
The rain had turned to ice.

The skies grew dark and the storms came in
And the sleet had turned to snow,
It covered all of the cliff-tops and
The sand on the cove below,
'We're in for a wicked winter,' I
Remarked, as I chopped the wood,
And she had turned, to give me a smile
To say that she understood.

The weeks went by and the storms still came
Til the cove had turned to ice,
The sea froze out in the distant bay
While we passed the time with dice,
'Isn't it strange how fate decrees,' she said
'How love will lie…
What if it wasn't Charlie, what
If it was you and I?'

The look on my face betrayed me, for
She sat right back and stared,

A tear had caught at my eye, she said,
'Why didn't you say you cared?'
'I couldn't see how you'd care for me
Though I cherished you as a friend,
I knew you would set your sights on Charles
And leave me in the end.'

'You didn't give me the choice, you should
Have left it for me to choose,
Now it's a little too late for us,
What did you have to lose?'
She stomped on out to the balcony
Where the hail came down like rice,
And like a fool, I left her there
Til her tears had turned to ice.

I found her frozen, stuck to the rail
Where she stood and stared to sea,
I should have taken her in before
And she might have come to me,
But still she stands with her frozen hands
As a barque sails into the bay,
And Charles will see that she came to me;
What am I going to say?

The Actress

'She was always a bit of an actress,
I remember how she was,
Back in the days of the village plays
When she changed her name to Roz,
She wouldn't respond to Eileen since
The day that she made the switch,
In print, the head of the programme said:
'Roz plays the Wicked Witch!''

'She always got into the parts she played
And would practice night and day,
Try to get into the head, she said
Of the character she'd play,
She'd wander round in a velvet gown
Or strip right down for the beach,
There wasn't a beach for twenty miles
But she'd towel herself in the street.'

'It must have become a way of life,
A habit, hard to break,
And went on after I'd married her
Though it brought its own heartache,
She had affairs with her leading men
But she saw no fault in this,
She said, 'It has to be genuine,
To portray authentic bliss!''

'The years went on and the parts she played
They became more grim and dour,
She'd often play the neglected wife
And her mood at home was sour,

She'd even try to attack me with
The words from her latest play,
And I would have to remind her that:
'My name's not Robin Day!''

'She rarely thought to apologise,
She said that she saw no need,
For after all, she was following
The muse of the artist's creed,
I tried to ignore the worst of it
When she flung both pots and pans,
But had to go off to the hospital
When she stomped on one of my hands.'

'She asked me to drive her out one night
To the cliffs at Beachy Head,
And play the part of a kidnapper
Who was holding a maid in dread,
She played her part, hung over the cliff,
And begged, and screamed, and stomped,
While I just said the word in the script
And the word in the script was 'Jump!''

'I didn't think she would jump, My Lord,
To me it was just a play,
To her it was the way that she lived,
Authentic in every way.
She screamed the most blood-curdling scream
That ever I heard, I know,
A scream that would bring the curtain down
On any top London show!'

The Circle Line

I'd driven a bus for thirty years
At least, for more than a spell,
But now I was getting on a bit
And I wasn't feeling well.
I'd taken a couple of sickies off
Well, more than I used to do,
And told the boss I would be okay,
It was just a dose of the flu.

But a note was waiting when I got back
All typed on a letterhead,
The company logo was large and black
And gave me a sense of dread.
I had to report to the man upstairs,
Way up on the twentieth floor,
I'd never been past the tenth for years,
Or called to account before.

I couldn't afford to lose my job,
Cut off at my time of life,
How would I pay the mortgage, then
Explain myself to the wife?
But I took the lift as I had to do,
And stood at a big black door,
Shivered there as I felt the chill
In the long, dark corridor.

A voice said 'Come!' and I wandered in
To an office of oak and teak,
The air was heavy with sandalwood
And I waited for him to speak.

He shuffled the papers on his desk
And his eyes flashed red, like fire,
'You've been a driver for thirty years,
Perhaps it's time to retire?'

My heart dropped into my boots at that,
I babbled that I was fine,
I couldn't retire for ten more years
If it pleased, I'd do my time.
He raised an eyebrow and pursed his lips
And I shook in my shoes with dread,
'We'll have to give you an easier route
On The Circle Line, instead.'

I'd heard bad things of the Circle Line
That the drivers didn't last,
I'd seen so many that came and went
On The Circle Line in the past.
'That's it, it's either The Circle Line
Or…' (the rest he left unsaid),
I thanked him quickly and turned to leave,
Relieved of my former dread.

The lift shot down to the basement where
There waited a big black bus,
A tall conductor approached me then:
'I see that you're joining us!'
I took my seat and I drove it out,
The conductor pointed the way,
'There's only twenty-one stops to make,
Just twenty-one stops today!'

We made a stop at the hospital
And the staff there loaded two,

Then carried on to the city jail
Where a man's parole was due,
They seemed subdued when they climbed aboard
And nobody even spoke,
Each face was pale as they held the rail,
They seemed to be anxious folk.

The route was finished within the hour
And I said to the man, 'Now where?'
He pointed out a lake on the map,
'We're dropping them all down there.'
I drove us into a quarry that
Was sitting beside the lake,
And found a monstrous entranceway
To a cave, he said, 'Now brake!'

A light was dancing, there in the cave,
Was flickering light and dark,
I said, 'Is that a fire in there?'
He answered, 'Merely a spark!'
He pushed the passengers off the bus
And led them into the cave,
To those that tried to resist, he said,
'It's a better place than the grave!'

The panic hit me as panic does
When you get a glimpse of the truth,
I may be old but I catch on fast,
Not like when I was a youth.
The bus I drove had a seven up
In front of the sign, as well,
And then I knew that the Circle Line
Was the Seventh Circle of Hell!'

I took the bus in a squealing turn
And I drove right out of the pit,
I left that tall conductor behind
For he was just part of it.
I dropped the bus in the nearby lake
And I walked back home to the wife,
A job's a job, but I'd rather take
A little bit more of life.

The Prince in the Garden Shed

I'd see strange lights in the garden shed
When I'd wake in the early hours,
Hanging out of the bedroom window,
Blowing smoke at the stars,
I wasn't allowed to smoke inside
So I'd hang out over the sill,
Whenever I'd wake at three o'clock
With the world so quiet and still.

Light would stream from a dozen cracks
Where the timber didn't fit,
The beams would light up the garden beds
With the rest of the patch unlit.
I'd listen hard for a movement there
But without the bedroom light,
Though nothing stirred in the shed out there
But the silence of the night.

To tell the truth I was just too scared
To go down and investigate,
The lights went off at four o'clock
On the dot, and never late,
I'd wait a while and go back to bed
But I very rarely slept,
While Constance lay with her back to me
As her innocence was kept.

I didn't tell her about the lights
Or admit that I sneaked a smoke,
She'd simply say that I drank too much
Or get mad, when she awoke,

But I checked the shed in the morning light
And opened the creaking door,
There were just a few old gardening tools
And a broken down lawnmower.

One night, I slept much longer than most
And I woke at half-past three,
But Constance wasn't there in the bed,
She wasn't where she should be.
I hung on out of the window then
And looked on down at the beams,
Where Constance was approaching the shed,
Asleep in her walking dreams.

She stopped, and opened the creaking door
Then she disappeared inside,
I held my breath and I lit a smoke
And a second one, beside.
I thought that she might have woken up
For the beams were still as bright,
But she only came when I called her name,
Still sleep-walking in the night.

She climbed back into our bed again
And slept the sleep of the dead,
She didn't wake until ten o'clock,
At breakfast then, I said:
'How did you sleep then, Constance dear,
You are somewhat flushed in the cheeks.'
She smiled a mystery smile: 'That was
The best that I've slept in weeks!'

'You didn't get up in the night,' I said,
'Imagine some lights, and beams?'

'No, I was lost in some palace, Ted,
And having the strangest dreams.
A prince sat high on a silver throne
But the air in there was a fog,
There was just the prince and myself alone,
But he had the head of a frog!'

She laughed, as never I'd heard her laugh,
And her eyes, they sparked with fun,
I couldn't believe the change in her,
She's never a happy one.
'I suppose that he asked to kiss you then
Like the tale from the Brothers Grimm?'
'Something like that,' said Constance,
But her lips were pursed, and prim.

It happened again another night
When I woke to find her gone,
She didn't come back at four o'clock,
Nor 'til the sun had shone.
I stopped her as she was walking back
But her eyes were wide awake,
'Don't even ask,' she said to me,
'Or you'll cause us both heartache.'

It's seven long months since they went out,
The lights in the garden shed,
And Constance cries when she tries to sit,
She says it's the baby's head,
She told me she doesn't want me there
When she's finally giving birth,
So I took an axe to the garden shed
And I piled the wood on the hearth!

The Rival

The hills were awash with winter rain
As I walked on down to the cross,
My coat was drenched and my feet were wet
As I thought of my recent loss.
The sun was hidden behind the clouds
When I got to the crossroads there,
And a single sliver of lightning flashed,
Shed light on my own despair.

I knew that I'd get there early, so
I sheltered under a tree,
They'd not set off from the market place
At least, 'til after three.
I should have come down in a coach and four
And kept right out of the rain,
But to freeze on the muddied bridle-path
Seemed to cauterize my pain.

It gave me time to adjust my mind
For the deed that had to be done,
Walk down the Hall of Remembrance for
A love that had been hard won,
The eyes that sparkled and smiled for me
Each time that I came in view,
Oh Caroline, sweet Caroline,
I'd have given the world for you!

That terrible night on the balcony
When you fought with Emily Krause,
You said she'd uttered some infamy
I should throw her out of the house.

I'd only left for an instant then
To recruit some help downstairs,
But when I returned to the balcony
She welcomed me back with a curse.

She said that you'd jumped, were in a rage,
She said that you'd had a fall,
She said that you'd gone, and I could gauge
That she was the best of all.
She backed away, and fell to her knees
While I stared down at the Mall,
She begged and sobbed, and she whispered 'Please!'
But you lay there in a sprawl.

The cart is pulled by a single horse
As it ambles down from the town,
She's dressed herself in a bonnet of blue
And worn her second-best gown.
A line of townsfolk follow it down
And they pelt her with refuse,
She screams with fear and I can but hear
Her say, 'Please cut me loose.'

The crossroads are a terrible place
With a sign that points to town,
The single arm that is braced in place
Has a rope burn, up and down,
I clamber up on the ancient cart
And I check that her hands aren't loose,
'Not you, my love, not you, by God!'
As I place her neck in the noose.

The Wishing Well

We'd bought a cottage, but sight unseen
At the edge of a thickety wood,
We'd had enough of the city scene
And thought it would do us good.
At one with nature, with birds and bees,
The owner was eager to sell,
He didn't tell us it had no power,
And water was drawn from a well.

He wouldn't leave us his new address
So we saw it after he'd gone,
I looked at Ellie and she at me,
She said, 'I think we've been done!'
The thatch was leaking, the walls were cracked
And it needed a coat of paint,
'Oh well, we're stuck with it now,' I said,
'But a palace it certainly ain't!'

The one surprise was a fairy dell
That lay at the edge of the wood,
And in the midst was a Wishing Well,
Under a Witch-Hat hood.
A wooden bucket was still in place
And hung from an oakum thread,
'We'd better replace the rope on that,
Or you'll be fishing,' she said.

The ground was covered in bluebells, for
They bloomed, that time of the year,
And all around them were butterflies,
Testing their wings in the air.

'Oh Jack,' she said, 'what a dainty place,
What a marvellous, magical scene,'
I had to admit, it moved me then,
So different to where we'd been.

We roughed it there for a day or so
While I fixed a couple of leaks,
I hinged the door and I blocked the draughts
Though the cracks would take me weeks.
We bought an antique paraffin lamp
For a little light in the gloom,
And lay on cushions that Ellie brought,
Made love on the floor of the room.

The water level within the well
Was high with the Springtime rain,
I only dipped the bucket a foot
To fill it with iced champagne,
The water there was so pure and clear
And cold, from the Wishing Well,
I said, 'This couldn't be water, Ell,
It's more like a fine Moselle.'

We worked by day, then we sat and read
In the pale white evening light,
Then rose with the early morning sun
After a dreamless night.
But after a fortnight Ellie rose
And she said she was feeling queer,
I said it was probably just a bug,
'It's the flu time of the year!'

But the pains, she said, got worse, she said,
She began to sweat and grieve,

She couldn't eat, but she drank a lot,
And then she began to heave.
I fed her the water from the well
And said it would flush it out,
But she soon went into convulsions,
And I panicked then, no doubt.

The doctor took over an hour to come
And that must have sealed her fate,
For Ellie lay, and she breathed her last
As he entered the garden gate.
He took one look at her pale white face
As I wept, and held her hand,
'I think it's a case of cholera,'
He said, 'Do you understand?'

The white coats swarmed all over the place
And took in the Wishing Well,
Wanted to know if we drank from it
And I cried out, 'God in Hell!
They grappled down to the very depths
And their hook was jagged at the bed,
Then hauled on up to the surface by
The hair, was a woman's head!

She'd been down there for a month or so,
Was starting to come apart,
The rest they got the following day
And took away on a cart.
I drained the well in the Autumn, and
I filled, with gravel and shell,
I should have known by the Witches-Hat
It was under an evil spell.

They caught the guy in another state,
They fairly ran him to ground,
He hadn't left a forward address,
He thought he'd never be found.
He'd killed his wife and had weighed her down
And had dropped her down in the well,
I pray to the God of just rewards
That his soul will burn in Hell!

The Devil's Drop Inn

The Inn he kept at the crossroads shone
A lantern, out on the street,
The only sign it was still alive
To the few its doors would greet,
Its passageway was in shadow once
You entered and closed the door,
And that was the way he wanted it,
The owner, Titus Claw.

For Titus was a hideous man
With a face like a railway wreck,
A scar cut deep with the fleshy burn
From a rope around his neck,
They said he'd cheated the hangman twice
With a neck like a coiled spring,
They'd hung on each of his legs in vain
For he never felt a thing.

The rope had broken under the strain
And dropped them all on the floor,
And he was the first to rise again
As he croaked, 'I'm Titus Claw!'
They backed away as his form had swayed
With the hood still over his head,
'There isn't a rope can cope with me,
If there was, then I'd be dead!'

They tried again, he began to spin
As the rope became undone,
The strands unravelling faster than
The ropemaker had spun,

The hangman turned and he crossed himself
As he said, 'I'm done with him!
If you want to hang this miserable wretch
Go find the Brothers Grimm!'

The Warden suffered a heart attack,
The jailers fled when they saw,
The Judge hid under the drop and cried,
'He's surely the Devil's spore!
Release him now so our souls are safe
From the reach of the evil one,
It's not his time for an early grave,
But God help everyone!'

So Titus went to manage the place
He called 'The Devil's Drop Inn',
That sat way out on the crossroads
With a sign that creaked in the wind,
Whole families would avert their eyes
As they passed, and cross themselves,
For the only patrons came by night
And they called them, 'Satan's Elves'.

They came with their hats pulled over their eyes,
Their collars hiding their cheeks,
Then slide on into the passageway
And wouldn't come out for weeks,
No lights were seen through the pebble glass
For the insides lay in gloom,
No drunken revellers came outside
It was silent as the tomb.

But once a month when the Moon was full
And the wind soughed up in the eaves,

A passer-by might hear a cry
Or a howl on the midnight breeze,
But nobody thought to check inside
They'd wear their hood like a cowl,
Then turn and suddenly rush away
When they heard an animal growl.

The storms would come and rattle the tiles,
As the sign would swing and creak,
And hail would shatter the window panes,
Three times in a week,
Til one dark shuddering winter's night
With the good folk in their cots,
The lightning struck on the Devil's peak
And shattered the chimney pots.

The fire began in the topmost room
And it raced on down the stair,
Gobbling up the dry rot that
It found most everywhere.
It made its way to the basement 'til
The whole Inn was ablaze,
The pebble glass was exploding
And the walls themselves were razed.

A couple of passers-by have sworn
That all they saw were cats,
Rushing out of the passageway
And followed by tawny rats,
But in the glow of the embers, heading
Over the hill, they saw,
A shadowy figure, slinking away
The image of Titus Claw!

Lost!

There's a glow in the sky this morning,
A pink, red-tinted glow,
But what will I do with the day to come,
I really wouldn't know,
You left on your final journey
When the night was still at last,
And everything that we knew and loved
Has now become the past.

I woke to the timbers creaking in
Our old house by the lake,
All else, a deafening silence
When you should have been awake.
I turned to you in our marriage bed
And I said, 'I'm feeling old!'
But you lay still in the morning chill
And God, but your hands were cold!

What will I tell the children?
What will I tell our friends?
You left with never a word for me
Or a chance to make amends.
I didn't think that the day would come
When you'd turn, and leave me blind,
But I awoke to the morning glow
And you'd left me far behind.

What will I do with the days ahead
As your figure fades from view,
With all the memories gone at last
Of the years that I spent with you?

I can't imagine a single day
When I'll never hear you speak,
As I kiss your lips and your fingertips
And my tears fall on your cheek.

The Sin Eater

It was after the funeral service
In the church at Calder Rise,
Hoping to catch a final glimpse
Of you, where your coffin lies,
I'd waited until the others left
And the church was quiet and still,
Then crept on round to the vestry door
And felt a sudden chill.

The coffin lay unattended on
The bier, by the font,
But someone was standing over it
Not someone that you'd want,
He raised the lid and he looked on down
Where you lay in your wedding dress,
Then reached on over your folded arms
And placed some bread on your breast.

He bowed his head and he muttered words
Of some Slavic, Eastern State,
I wanted to interrupt him, but
By then, it was too late,
He took the bread and he wolfed it down
And gagged on the slice of rye,
And as he did, your body heaved
In the coffin, and gave a sigh.

'My God,' I gasped, as I staggered in,
'What awful thing have you done?
What spell could possibly interfere
With death, but an evil one?'
He turned to me, was taken aback
That I'd seen the thing he did,
'Don't mess with what you don't understand,'
He said, then closed the lid.

He started to walk back up the aisle
But he choked, then doubled up,
He started having convulsions
Then his face became corrupt,
His brow was furrowed, his jaw was locked
With his mouth, an evil grin,
'I've taken away her path to Hell,'
He groaned, 'I've eaten her sin!'

While back on the bier the coffin lay,
Began to open its lid,
And you sat up in your shroud of death
And fluttered each dead eyelid,
You stared at me with a great intent
And muttered, with words like ice,
'He's eaten the sin of you and I,
So meet me in paradise!'

Your corpse collapsed on the coffin's side,
Your arms were reaching for me,
I backed away in a panic then
And hid in the church vestry,
We'd lain together the month before
And the sin was deep in my heart,

The Sin-Eater was dead on the floor,
My guilt would tear me apart.

I knew I would have to cleanse my soul
If you were to meet with me,
Though you were headed for paradise
I didn't know where I'd be,
I came again when the church was dark
And knelt, where the man was dead,
Crossed myself, and I laid it down
On his chest, a slice of bread.

The End of Faery

Garth lay still in the gilded cage
Unable to move a thing,
The bars were merely spiders' webs
Of a faery's magicking.
He'd wandered into the Faery Ring
Where he'd seen the mushrooms spread,
And now was caught in a faery spell
With the rest of the living dead.

With Tom, the Candlestick Maker's son
And a barrel of candlewax,
He'd dawdled home from the marketplace
And lay in the beckoning grass.
He woke to find he was tightly bound
With a faery up on his chest,
She said, 'Lock him in the cage as well,
Along with all of the rest.'

And Madge, the maid with a milking pail
Who was sent to milk the cow,
She'd wandered off on her way; she thought,
She needed to feed the sow.
She woke to mushrooms, ten feet tall
All towering over her head,
The stalks were bars, set under the stars
And her limbs, they felt like lead.

While Tim the Tinker was there as well
With his knives and sharpening tools,
His grindstone lay in a pile of hay
And the bonds on him were cruel.

The beggar lay in his filthy rags
While the rich man muttered, 'Shame!'
He'd soiled his boots and his Regency suit,
Was bound with his watch and chain.

They lie not far from the caravans
Of a gypsy camping ground,
So Faeries say: 'Let's take them away
Before they're seen and found!'
But dancing into the faery ring
Is the Gypsy, Mavourneen,
Who stumbles over the gilded cage
And steps on the Faery Queen.

The top flies off from the gilded cage,
The webs of the bars are torn,
And Garth crawls over the mushroom heads
To swear, 'I feel reborn!'
The faeries weep as they carry their Queen
In death, to their Faery Dell,
There's mushrooms still in that Faery Ring,
But now, Toadstools as well!

Crow!

The wind was swaying the treetops as
I cut across from the church,
The sun had darkened behind the clouds
When I saw the crow on its perch,
Its feathers fluttered, it looked quite grim
As it sat there, quite on its own,
But watching me with a beady eye
From the top of a blank headstone.

I pulled the collar around my ears
And hunched in my overcoat,
The wind was bringing a bitter chill
To whip at my face and throat,
I staggered over and off the path,
Walked over the headstone plot,
And felt a shiver run down my spine
To wonder what time she'd got.

The crow had uttered a single 'caw'
From the depths of its blue-black beak,
Then spread its wings like an avatar
And lashed a gash in my cheek,
I stumbled off, I could feel the blood
As it ran, from under my eye,
And hurried home, though I flung a stone
At the crow as it flew on by.

But Rachel stood at the window as
I came in the gate, at last,
She saw the blood, and she put her hand
On up to her mouth, aghast.

I told her it was a minor cut
A thorn on a rose that waved,
She shuddered, flooded her eyes with tears,
Said, 'Someone walked on my grave!'

'Someone walked on my grave,' she said
'Not even an hour ago…'
My mind went back to the headstone, and
The evil glare of the crow.
'You're overwrought, you should sit and rest,
Get warm, for the room is dank,'
But all I could see in my mind just then
Was a headstone that was blank.

I'd taken her from a cruel home
For her parents both were dead,
She'd been brought up by a grandmother
Who was violent, sick she said.
She'd threatened me when we went away
That she'd not be long my bride,
And Rachel never felt safe with me
'Til her grandmother had died.

I managed to catch the warden when
I saw him, late in the week,
'Why is that headstone blank?' I said,
'Whose is the grave you keep?'
'There's no-one buried under that stone,
It was raised for a future soul,
A woman came in the driving rain
And paid for that grave with gold.'

'But surely you have a name for her
In the graveyard book; you'd know.'

He knitted his brow, and thought aloud:
'I think that her name was Crow!
She dressed in black, in a mourning gown
With a cloak that looked like wings,
Then vanished, as she had first appeared
When I turned to ask her things.'

I passed the stone on the way back home,
And I stared, my mouth ajar,
For someone had cut a letter there
In the face of the stone, an 'R',
I thought of Rachel, hurried on home
But was late, too late I know,
For flying past as I reached the gate
Was the dread form of the crow.

It crashed straight into the window where
My Rachel stood and stared,
Dressed in black, in a mourning gown
It was just as I had feared.
The window smashed as the crow had crashed
With shards of glass all round,
The crow embedded in Rachel's throat
As she choked her last on the ground.

She lay with both of her arms outstretched
Like a pair of wings in black,
The bird ripped open her jugular,
She wouldn't be coming back.
I knew she'd hated her grandmother,
She remembered every blow,
But didn't think she'd be coming back
Though her maiden name was 'Crow!'

Next Time Around

I'd come back home from an early shift
When I wasn't expected - True!
But the house on the hill was cold and still
So I went off, looking for you.
I couldn't find you at your parents place,
They said they hadn't a clue,
Your brother said he'd not seen your face
Since the day we spent at the zoo.

It wasn't like you to disappear,
You might have left me a note,
It wasn't until I came back home
That I found one, stuffed in my coat.
'I've gone to the place that dreamers go
When the world is getting them down,
Gone where a dreamer's dreams would seem
To be better, next time around.'

My heart flipped once and it almost stopped,
I'd thought we were doing well,
We'd been together for seven years
I was truly caught in your spell.
I'd thought that your air of discontent
Was a phase, but I couldn't see,
You left on the first full day of Lent
So you were giving up me!

I wandered around our empty house
For days, in the throes of grief,
I felt my heart had been torn apart,
Then I thought of my cousin, Keith.

He'd lodged with us for a month or so
And I'd seen the spark in his eyes,
But barely noticed the answering glow
Of your own, so now - Surprise!

I found a bundle of letters then
In the back of your bedside drawer,
From him to you and from you to him,
I'd never looked there before.
They spilled their passion on every page
Like a toadstool, spreading its spore,
His love was greater than mine, he said,
He'd love you forevermore.

And you said terrible things of me
That I'd treated you with neglect,
That I'd taken your love for granted, and
Was an albatross round your neck.
I couldn't believe the things I read
From the one that I'd loved to death,
But now, I knew what you really said
With every disloyal breath.

You'd slept with him while I went to work,
He'd never worked in his life,
But like a Judas he'd worked his will
On you, a deceitful wife.
My stomach turned and I felt quite sick,
For days, it tumbled and churned,
The pain in my heart was like a brick
Til the day that my anger burned.

* * * * * * *

A month went by and she came again
To knock at our own front door,
'I've made an awful mistake,' she said
As her tears ran down on the floor.
'I'll do whatever it takes,' she said,
'To make the pain go away.'
My eyes were sad but my heart was glad
As I said what I had to say.

'I've gone to the place that dreamers go
When the world is getting them down,
Gone where a dreamer's dreams would seem
To be better, next time around.
I haven't a place in my life for you
Since you left with such little grace,'
Then I shook my head, for my love was dead
And I slammed the door in her face.

Key to the Door

They said she suffered from visions, so
They locked her up in her room,
I heard her pacing the floor in there
To softly cry in the gloom,
Her food they slid in under the door
And that's when I heard her shout:
'You can't keep me forever in here,
You must let my nightmares out!'

But a doctor listened outside the door
And shook his head as he went,
A Priest then wafted some incense in
And muttered a sacrament,
But no-one dared to unlock the door
For they'd heard a howl within,
'She must be conjuring demons there
Or some terrible type of sin.'

At night when everyone was asleep
I'd put my head to the floor,
And whisper low to my sister through
The gap, just under the door.
'Go find the key,' she would say to me,
'And unlock the door in the night,
We'll creep on out while the house is still,
Take off while the Moon is bright.'

I didn't know where to find the key,
I didn't know where it was,
It wasn't hung up on the kitchen hook
Or the nail in the wooden cross.

She begged me, 'Keep on looking for it,
It's the only chance for me,
Then we will be together again
At last, and finally free!'

But then her visions returned again
And lights shone under the door,
While sounds, like animals caught in pain
Built up to a sullen roar.
I whispered, 'Sis, can you hear me now,
I'm scared,' and started to bawl,
She cried, 'There's lights and a million things
All creeping out of the wall.'

I went to beat on our parent's door
But I heard my father snore,
I ran downstairs and I found the key
They'd hid in the bureau drawer.
I hesitated before I turned
The key in my sister's lock,
The door swung open and lay ajar
As I stood, stock-still in shock.

For in the room was a wooded glade
With creepers clogging the walls,
Bats were hung from the old lampshade,
The bed was a waterfall,
But of my sister, never a sign
She must have been lost in the trees,
But monsters struggled out of the wall
As I fell in dread to my knees.

They say I suffer from visions, so
They've locked me up in my room,

I couldn't cope with my sister's loss
They said, but she's in a tomb.
I know she's not, for I hear her whisper
Under the door at night,
'We'll creep on out while the house is still,
Take off while the Moon is bright.'

Then sounds, like animals caught in pain
Build up to a sullen roar,
I call for her, again and again,
'Just get the key to the door.'
But then she fades, and she slips away,
So far that I have to shout:
'You can't keep me forever in here,
You must let my nightmares out!'

Topsy Turvy

Samantha worked in the Take-away
Right next to the Coalpit Mine,
With a cheery smile for everyone
Til the day that her eyes went blind.
One minute she served up fish and fries
Then her world went eerie and dark,
'Has the sun gone suddenly down,' she said,
'Behind the trees in the park?'

They called me back from my p.m. shift
For they knew that we two were close,
She'd dated some other miners too
But she'd gone with me the most.
'You'd better get her on home,' they said,
'There's something wrong with her eyes,'
She stared in a peculiar way
With a vacant look of surprise.

The doctor said there was nothing wrong,
Or nothing that he could see,
'It must be something psychological,'
That's what he said to me.
He flashed a light in each of her eyes
But she didn't even wince,
I must admit, it troubled me less
Than events that happened since.

I said perhaps we should get engaged
Rather than take it slow,
I'd be her eyes and a steady guide
Wherever she'd need to go,

She smiled that wonderful smile at me
And said, 'You need to be sure,
You're tying yourself to an invalid
Who can't venture out the door.'

We bought the ring at a jeweller's shop
Where she chose the ring by feel,
A tiny diamond, glittered and shone,
She asked if the stone was real.
We laughed as I guided her back home
And she clung on tight to my arm,
I swore that I would protect her then,
And stop her coming to harm.

A week went by, and I took my leave
From the dirt and dust of the mine,
We laughed and loved and said together
That things would work out fine,
But then I noticed a subtle change
In the way that the house was laid,
The rooms seemed somewhat bigger than ever
The architects had made.

The chairs and tables would move about
From one day to the next,
I asked Samantha what she had done
And she answered, 'Nothing yet!'
She didn't trip and she didn't fall
As I did, the fault was mine,
I had two eyes but I couldn't gauge
The depths of Samantha's mind.

She said she had to rebuild her world,
Recall from her memory,

And if it wasn't exactly right
It wouldn't matter to me.
'You have two eyes, you can navigate,
While I'm still trapped in the dark,
I still remember that day of fate
When the sun blinked out in the park.'

We opened the door to venture out
And I blinked, and gave a grunt,
The supermarket was on the right
With everything back to front.
'The mine was off in the east,' I said,
'But now it's off to the west.'
Samantha shrugged, 'Does it matter now?
You'll see, it's all for the best.'

She walked as if she had perfect sight,
While I just followed behind,
My head was spinning in horror at
Each different thing that we'd find.
And people stood, and stared in the street
As if in a total daze,
They turned and twisted and took it in
This mirror glimpse of their ways.

'You have to set it to rights,' I said,
'You have to turn it around.
The people here will be going mad
At what you've done to their town!'
'They'll have to adjust,' Samantha shrugged
As she went to step off the kerb,
Just as a double-decker bus
Came round the corner and swerved.

'The road was suddenly back to front,'
The driver said, as he cried,
'I had to get back over the line,'
He said, as Samantha died.
We live in a topsy-turvy world
In thrall to the power of mind,
When anything can that happen will…
(I hope I never go blind!)

The Yellow Doll

I'd known Dionne since her coming out
In a dress of tulle, in cream,
And held my breath when she took the floor
To glide like an autumn dream.
My eyes had followed her, all that night
As she danced from hand to hand,
I knew from then I would be in thrall,
She became my promised land.

She married badly the first time, and
I thought that she'd come to me,
She leapt from the fat of the frying pan
To the fire of the Presbytery,
Her husband Sol gave his sermons on
The fires in the pit of Hell,
Eternal moans in a fire of bones
With a terrible brimstone smell.

She seemed subdued, in a sullen mood
When I went to tea one day,
I asked her if she was happy now
But she simply looked away.
I saw a tear on her dainty cheek
And it took me by surprise,
'I'm such a fool,' she revealed to me,
'I should have been more than wise.'

She said she wished she had never wed
For the first had made her cry,
He'd come home drunk for a solid month
And she said, she'd wondered why.

'I loved him then, and I slaved for him
For I thought that he loved me too,
But then I heard about Annabelle,
And she, just one of a few.'

She married, after a swift divorce
A man with a flinty soul,
'So much different to Adam, he
Is true, but his love is cold.
He tortures me with his tales of Hell,
Of sin in this earthly place,
And threatens that I might meet him there
If I don't live in God's Grace.'

She told me about a yellow doll
That she'd had since she was four,
She'd lavished love and affection on
But she didn't, anymore.
He'd burnt its hands and he'd burnt its feet
When he'd been annoyed with her,
And said that she was the yellow doll,
The devil was waiting for.

I told her that she should leave him
That the man must be insane,
And told her that I would take her home,
That I would bear the blame.
She smiled at me with her sad blue eyes
And she said, 'You're really sweet,
But he has threatened to hunt me down
If he sees me in the street.'

She said he'd threatened to burn her feet
As he'd done, the yellow doll,

She'd not be able to walk again
And leave him, like a trull.
I left that day with a heavy heart
But at least, I knew the score,
Though when I tried to return again
I found that he'd barred the door.

The months went by and I thought of her
For she never left my head,
But then one day came the welcome news,
It seemed that he was dead.
I stood well back at the funeral
And I watched the widow's face,
Under the flimsy widow's veil
She shone with an inner grace.

We kept apart for a month or two
But I knew that she was mine,
We tried to avoid a scandal, it
Was just a question of time,
We married after a year had gone
He'd long been in the ground,
We couldn't believe the harmony
And the love that we had found.

But then on a cold, black winter's day
Dionne cried out aloud,
For beating hard on the cedar door
There was someone in a shroud,
And lying there on the welcome mat
Lay the little yellow doll,
Its feet were totally charred and black
And Dionne cried out, 'It's Sol!'

She clung to me and was petrified
And I tried to calm her down,
'It can't be Sol, for you saw him planted
Six feet under the ground.'
The shroud continued to beat the door
And Dionne, her voice was grim,
She pointed to the doll on the floor,
'I buried the doll with him!'

Shooting Star

I followed her over the countryside,
I followed her near and far,
She said that she had to live her life
Alone, as a shooting star.
'The world began when I came to be
Will be gone,' she began to shout,
'When I leave my trail, a silvery tail
And the Moon and the stars go out.'

'But what about love,' I called to her
As she shimmied by in the breeze,
Her eyes were fixed on the future as
I settled down on my knees.
'I haven't got time for love,' she said
'It fades, and swallows my life,
There's more to living what I've been given
Than being somebody's wife.'

'The world out there is a lonely place
When you wander its wilds alone,
You'll need somebody to hold your hand
In the dark, when you're on your own.'
'I don't need someone to tie me down
I shall steer my course for me,
No man shall tug at my either hand
Or change my trajectory.'

'My heart is full of my love for you,'
I said, but she didn't care,
She laughed, and hurried away to find
What life had in store for her.

I caught a sight of her now and then
As she lived her life to the full,
With greedy lips at the brimming cup
As she drained the life from her soul.

The years were cruel as she partied on,
Her hair became iron grey,
Her skin was losing that youthful bloom
With the drugs that she took each day,
The money lenders were out in force
So she had to swallow her pride,
And sell herself when she had to pay,
But then she shrivelled inside.

She landed up on my doorstep only
Once, and I thought she'd fall,
She looked so ill that my heart went out
But my skin began to crawl,
'So what became of the shooting star?'
I said - She began to pout,
Then tears welled up at her eyelids as
Her Moon and her stars went out.

Black & White

I sat up late with a Shoot-em-up
While the wife went off to bed,
There was a time I'd have joined her, but
She only had sleep in her head.
There was Gabby Hayes and a guy called Clint
Holed up in a barn, in Mo.,
And blasting away at the barn outside
Was an evil guy, called Joe.

I knew which was the good and the bad
Though they each wore a Stetson hat,
For Hayes and Clint's were a pearly white
While this evil Joe's was black.
He'd robbed the Stage, and hidden the loot
In the barn, where the good guys lay,
He yelled, 'You'd better throw out them sacks,
If not, then you'd better pray!'

'The Sheriff will come and kick your butt,'
Rang out the voice of Clint,
'I'll say, Dadburned if he don't,' said Hayes
'You're a pesky, bad varmint!'
Then it ended, as the old westerns did
With Joe laid out on a slab,
Though he starred again in a hundred films
He was always labelled bad.

I went out onto the porch to smoke
It was warm, a summer night,
While the Southern Cross shone up above
In the Milky Way, so bright,

And I pondered then on a single line
That Joe had snarled, to connive,
'If you don't throw out them sacks right now
You'll never get out alive!'

The world is full of the likes of Joe
Who threaten and rob, and steal,
While the rest of us are lying low
And living a life that's real.
But he said one thing that applies to us
To the bad and the good that strive,
Whatever the sort of life you live
You'll never get out alive!'

The Living Dead

I pass my time with the living dead
As I sit in my home, alone,
As spectres range through my fevered head,
I don't have a telephone,
I tend to avoid the world out there
And the folk who pass in the street,
So only go out in the night to roam
And hope that we'll never meet.

The world, to me, is an empty place
By the light of the gas-lamp glow,
I only roam historical streets
Of a hundred years or so,
My people walked in the streets and lanes
Where I drink my fill of the past,
The lives they lived, though over and done
Are the only ones that last.

I bury my head in ancient books
That tell of their living deeds,
The interactions and social factions
That answered most of their needs,
They come alive on the page to me
As I share their highs and lows,
Like Oscar Wilde with his sense of style
And the Edgar Allan Poes.

So many lives that were lived, then lost
That wouldn't have left a trace,
If someone hadn't written of them,
Had tried to capture each face,

Their words are part of our culture now
As some writer set them down,
And these, the writers are dead themselves
But their books are their renown.

A life is only ever complete
With the last and final breath,
We cease to be the man in the street,
The end of the book is death.
But life is there on the printed page
To entrance with what they said,
And I'm content to enrich my life,
To walk with the living dead.

Strange Encounter

He was sat in a quaint old country pub
And huddled over the fire,
The logs were blazing, spreading their heat
But the look on his face was dire.
There was only us on that winter's night
The regulars stayed away,
So I sat beside him to share the heat
And hear what he had to say.

The rain outside, pit-pattering down
Had flooded under the porch,
It was so pitch black in the night outside
That to leave, I'd need a torch.
So I settled in for a lengthy stay,
He said that his name was Jim,
The air of gloom in that empty room
Seemed to be coming from him.

I said, 'What's up?' and he looked at me
As if he was going to cry,
I said, 'It can't be as bad as that,'
But he let out an awful sigh.
'It's worse, far worse than you'd ever think,'
There followed a drawn-out pause,
But then he thought to confide in me,
'I'm going to get a divorce.'

'I see,' I said, and I let him talk,
He needed to get it out,
A man in pain, while the driving rain
Outside, meant he had to shout.

'I loved Elaine, and I never strayed,
Not once did I look aside,
For years Elaine was my universe
But now, it's a question of pride.'

'She told me she had a sister, who
Had needed a place to stay,
A Rosalyn, and she moved right in,
I thought she would go away.
But no, she stayed, and the sisters played
And I worked while they went to shop,
She came in between the two of us,
So I said that it had to stop.'

'I didn't think she would take her part
But she did, and pushed me away,
And that was the first of the arguments
We'd had, since our wedding day.
She'd throw a fit and would put me down,
It was messing with my head,
And then she would turn and leave the room,
And sleep in her sister's bed.'

'For months, I tried to ignore it, but
It gradually got me down,
She said I wasn't much fun these days,
That all that I did was frown,
So just last night in a fit of spite
I thought that I'd take a stand…
I burst on in through their bedroom door,
Her Rosalyn was a man!'

The Last Druid

She'd lived alone since her husband left
Just after the fall of Rome,
Deep in the forest she'd kept herself
In the tangle of trees called home.
He'd left with one of the Legions, they
Recalled to defend the State,
Leaving Britain with Roman roads
And her people, left to their fate.

Aeronwy came from a Druid clan
From a mixture of kings and gods,
She'd never age in the forest glade
Where she lived with her hunting dogs.
She lived on berries and lived on fruits
And the kill that the dogs brought in,
But knew she never must see herself
Reflected in any spring.

'For if you do,' said a holy man
'You will see that the years are fraught,
Your spells and philtres won't help you then,
You'll lose what the ancients taught.
The years will tumble over your breast
In a wave, and take your breath,
As long as you live in this vale of trees
You will be immune to death.'

She wept for the loss of her husband then
For he never came back home,
She didn't know he'd been taken off
With his Legion, back to Rome.

They'd met when a hunting party came
To slaughter her Druid clan,
But she was spared, for her beauty there
Would entrance most any man.

He'd stayed with her in the forest glade
For a month of making love,
She prayed that he'd never leave her, in
A plea to the gods above,
She little knew of the world out there
Of the waning Roman's might,
And so she wallowed in bitter tears
In her loneliness, each night.

Her time was not as the time for us,
Her minute was like our day,
The years would fly in her restless nights
As she dreamed her life away.
But she woke as fresh and as beautiful
As she'd been the night before,
While scores of agues and deadly plagues
Swept on, in a world at war.

The forest began to shrink as men
Fed wood to their kilns and fires,
What once had been a forest became
A wood, in the sight of spires,
She heard the clang of hammers on steel
At the factories rise and rise,
And soon her trees were surrounded by
New roads, and telephone wires.

Then men came into her forest glade
While cutting a new canal,

She hid in the corner, in the shade
As her trees began to fall.
One day she woke and the cut was there
With a little hump-backed bridge,
She mounted slowly, up to the top
And balanced over the edge.

She gazed down into the water that
Was still as a mirror's sheen,
And saw the face that began to race
Through the thousand years she'd seen.
Her hair flew wide, and before she died
She muttered a weary moan,
'I'd be content if it only meant
That my husband came back home!'

The Raggedy Man

Driving blind through a flurry of mist
On a road beyond the glare,
I'd left the hurrying city behind
For the peace of who knows where,
There wasn't a light on the country road
But a glimmer from the stars
Was high ahead where the road had led
To the faint red glow of Mars.

I'd had to get me away that day
Or I thought I'd go insane,
My life was sputtering in the gutter
And all it brought was pain.
I'd had my fill of the diesel fumes,
Of the cold, unloving ways,
The condescending, trivial chatter
That marked and maimed my days.

And she, the light of my underworld
With the flaming, golden hair,
Had gone with one of the chattering kind,
Had turned and left me there.
The lips that had whispered words of love
Way back, when our world was new,
Had now been pursed as my world was cursed
With her eyes, ice cold and blue.

My headlights, dim on the road ahead
Formed a short and rounded arc,
I couldn't peer past my inner fear
That my road ahead was dark.

The wind blew up and the rain came down
And it burst across the screen,
I couldn't see twenty yards ahead
So I questioned what I'd seen.

A sudden flash on the roadside there
Of a figure draped in rags,
That flapped and fluttered about his form,
A hat with a brim that sagged,
A paltry second I'd seen him there
Then gone, as the car swept by,
I sat in shock, and was taking stock,
Should I stop and help the guy?

I'd travelled almost a mile before
My conscience had got to me,
Then turned around and retraced the ground
Where I thought he'd surely be.
He stood alone in his flapping rags
As I turned the car around,
Glistening wet on the darkened road
He stood, not making a sound.

He wouldn't sit in the front with me
But sat in the back, and sighed,
'It's awful wet on the road tonight,
I thought that you'd like a ride.'
I saw him nod in the mirror then,
He just inclined his head,
But then I saw that his eyes were gone
And I felt a creeping dread.

The things that I thought were rags I saw
Were feathers, tightly sewn,

The feathers of some black, evil bird
That had once both soared and flown.
'I'm heading North, I can drop you off,
But you'll need to tell me when.'
He mumbled something I couldn't hear
And, 'I won't tell you again!'

His voice sent shivers all down my spine
For it croaked, just like a crow,
Rumbling up from some deep pit
Nightmares and phantoms know.
I kept one eye on the mirror then
As the sweat formed on my brow,
He seemed to sense I was more than tense,
'You mustn't be worried now.'

'I'm leading you to a future that
You'd possibly never find,
I wouldn't normally help you, but
You stopped, and were more than kind.'
He said to turn on a track ahead
And I did, but didn't know why,
Then saw a glimmer of light ahead,
The flames reached up to the sky.

A house was burning, the upper floor
Was bathed in an eerie glow,
I jumped on out of the car and went
To scour the floor below,
A girl lay pale on the kitchen floor
And I scooped her up where she lay,
Carried her out to the waiting car
As she woke, in a mute dismay.

The figure stood in the pouring rain
And rustled his feathered cape,
'Your future lies in your own hands now,
The past is yours to escape.
Be strong and true, it will come to you
That you'll never have to atone,'
His feathers fluttered, and then he flew,
Leaving us there alone.

When people ask how we came to meet
I always let out a groan,
While Amity says, 'That's a subject
That we think's best left alone.'
We might tell them of the burning house,
How I scooped her up from the floor,
But never mention the raggedy man,
His flight, or the clothes he wore.

Lobster Reef

An Isle rose up from the ocean swell
On the seventeenth of June,
It was totally unexpected by
The M.V. Cameroon,
She'd sailed with seven passengers
And some cargo in the hold,
They all kept well to their cabins for
The deck was more than cold.

The Captain up on the bridge had checked
His maps before they sailed,
Had marked his course dead reckoning
Though the gyro compass failed,
They'd been at sea for eleven days
So he took a fix on the stars,
Then left the wheel to the Bosun while
He searched for the coffee jar.

The ship ground up on a coral reef
At two in the morning, sharp,
The night was black as a midden since
The clouds had hidden the stars,
The hull bit deep in the coral as
It drove ahead with its way,
Grinding slowly to come to halt
Just in from a new-formed bay.

'There isn't supposed to be land out here,'
The Bosun cried to Lars,
The Captain said, 'I fixed a point,
Dead reckoning by the stars!

There shouldn't be land in a hundred miles,'
But the ship was high and dry,
'It must have come up from the ocean floor,'
The Bosun said, 'but why?'

The passengers spilled out onto the deck
With cries and shouts in the gloom,
'What have you done, the ship's a wreck,'
Said the Banker, Gordon Bloom.
The sisters, Jan and Margaret Young
Burst out in sobs and tears,
'How are you going to float it off?
We might be here for years!'

At daylight they could see the extent
Of the distant lava flow,
'Lucky we're not on the other side
Or we'd all be dead, you know.'
The tide came in and the tide went out
But the ship was high and dry,
As clouds of steam from the lava flow
Poured out, and into the sky.

'We're not gonna starve,' said Andy Hill
As he peered down onto the reef,
As thousands of crabs and lobsters crawled
'There's plenty of them to eat.'
They lowered him down on a rope, along
With the engineer, Bob Teck,
Where they gathered the lobsters up by hand
And tossed them, up on the deck.

The evening meal was a feast that night,
They ate and they drank their fill,

'Too much,' said Oliver Aston-Barr
'I think I'm going to be ill.'
But Jennifer Deane, Costumier
Had an appetite for four,
She ate the scraps that the others left
And was calling out for more.

The following morning all was still
Til Jennifer Deane came out,
She roused them all with a frightened scream,
And then continued to shout:
'I've got some horrible bug inside
And I've lost my sense of taste,
It must have come from the lobsters, for
It's eaten half of my face!'

The lobsters must have been undercooked
For the symptoms would appal,
A necrotizing flesh eater
Had started on them all.
The flesh was eaten from Andy's hand
And the leg of Gordon Bloom,
While the sisters Jan and Margaret Young
Lay screaming in their room.

The sickness took them rapidly,
For Jennifer Deane had died,
They had no place to bury her
So threw her over the side,
The crabs then swarmed and attacked her there,
Ate all of her flesh away,
There was little left of Jennifer Deane
Before the end of the day.

Each time that one of them died, the rest
Would fling them over the side,
The bodies had piled up higher out there
Than those alive, inside,
Til finally, Oliver Aston-Barr
Was last to die, on the bridge,
Of the Motor Vessel Cameroon,
Upthrust on a lava ridge.

A winter storm was to float it off,
It drifted out with the tide,
A rusted hulk with 'The Cameroon'
Paint peeling, off from the side.
An ancient freighter, crossing its path
Drove past it, steel on steel,
And that's when the helmsman held his breath,
'There's a skeleton at the wheel!'

The End of Motherly Love

We were friends of a sort, when we were young
When we grew, I thought he was weak,
Jumping at shadows in shady lanes,
At jokes that were tongue-in-cheek.
He thought that life was a trap for him
And looked for someone to blame,
He could have been so much more, I thought,
Than he was, and that was a shame.

His soul was timorous, that was true
But he seemed to attract the girls,
They'd give him a shoulder to cry on, when
He was feeling at odds with the world.
They called him 'Bobby', that said it all
When he should have been known as Bob,
He never grew to be Bob, I knew
But won their hearts with a sob.

He brought out the motherly instincts in
The girls that he got to know,
They would pet his hair, and say, 'There there…'
And motion for me to go.
My sweetheart, Carolyn Ainsworth said
That he'd won a place in her heart,
I couldn't believe she could be so dumb
But her interest tore us apart.

I watched as she moved on into his life
And catered for every whim,
He told me not to approach her then,
She was only there for him.

They moved on into a haunted house
On a plot, with a dog outside,
A wooden house with a creaky gate
Where her grandfather had died.

They married, out on their own front lawn
Then scurried away inside,
He wouldn't let her out of his sight
But clung to his captive bride.
I never saw her out on her own
He was always there, like a freak,
And pulled her in, like a dog on a leash
Whenever she tried to speak.

I got a note in the mail one day
That was signed by Carolyn,
'Please come and take me away,' it said,
'Oh, what a fool I've been!'
I drove on out to the haunted house
But the gate and the doors were barred,
Then she came on out to the balcony,
I could tell she was more than scared.

Her eye was blackened and bruised, I saw,
Her lip was swollen and split,
I called 'Come down!' and I waved to her,
'I'll take you away, my sweet!'
But Bobby came to the balcony
And he dragged her in by the hair,
The doors had slammed and I heard them lock,
And a terrible scream up there.

I vaulted over the creaky gate
And I kicked the front door in,

Then made for the central stair, but fate
Was putting paid to his sin.
A shadowy figure had seized him there
And thrust him against the wall,
Then sent him tumbling down the stairs,
He broke his neck in the fall.

It stood there, glaring down from the top
Then slowly faded away,
I'd never have met her grandfather
If I hadn't been there that day.
I took her home and I patched her up
But knew that my love had flown,
I see her now and again, she lives
With him in her haunted home.

The Whispering Wall

The Whispering Wall of Shah La Mere
Had drawn him over the hills,
They said that it only whispered truth
That the listening ear distils,
His lover stood at the further side
And whispered into the wall:
'I'd like to give you it all,' she said,
He heard, 'I wish you were Paul.'

They'd fashioned the Dam at Shah La Mere
Where the valley narrowed down,
To catch the tumbling waters there
When the winter floods came round,
The wall of the Dam was curved across
From the cliff on the western side,
And fixed to stone in the eastern zone
On the hill called 'Devil's Pride.'

A walkway followed the curve across
That was barely three feet wide,
A thousand feet from the valley floor
You could walk it, if you tried,
There wasn't a safety rail out there
For the faint of heart, or weak,
But those who needed to hear the truth
Would brave it, just to speak.

The whispers gathered and echoed there
At the centre of the curve,
And kept on muttering as you passed,
Trapped in the wall's reverb,

The Whisperers, long gone, were caught
In their whispers of lies and truth,
'I will be honest and true,' became,
'I'm still messed up with Ruth.'

Corinne stayed safe on the eastern side
While he walked out to the west,
They'd vowed their love to each other, then
Had thought to put it to test.
He passed the muttering echoes where
So many others had been,
The truth was turning to lies out there
With some of it quite obscene.

He stopped and turned on the other side
'Can you hear me now, Corinne?'
And she had nodded as she had heard
'Do you fear me, now and then?'
'I've only wanted to be with you,'
Was the whisper she returned,
'I'm only waiting for someone new,'
He heard, and his ears burned.

'They say it only whispers the truth,'
He muttered, his eyes cast down,
'I may be soon returning to Ruth,'
Was the whisper that came round.
He dropped her off at her mother's place
From their trip to the Whispering Wall,
Then drove at speed to spend time with Ruth
While she caught up with Paul.

The Last Friend

He stood at the back, and looked around
The church, not even full,
There wasn't a face he recognised
From his far off days at school,
He thought of Jim in the coffin there
Who had reached his end of days,
Then hid his head and the tears he shed
As they sang a hymn of praise.

The congregation had filed on out
To attend a hurried wake,
'I hope she finished the Lamingtons,'
Said the grandson, Edward Drake.
'We're lucky to have a wake at all
For they've been divorced for years,
I couldn't believe she'd put it on
But she even cried real tears!'

He didn't follow the mourners down
But turned away on his own,
He hadn't anything much to say
To the strangers Jim had known,
He'd said goodbye to his only friend
To the last one that he had,
The rest had gone on ahead of him
And the thought of that was sad.

What do you do in an empty world
When the last of those you knew
Is lying under a grassy knoll,
Covered in morning dew?

When your wife has gone to an early grave
And your son has gone, too soon,
While a daughter's taken in childbirth
Early one Sunday afternoon.

He walked and walked til the sun went down,
To the sound of an inner voice,
'Why have you stayed around so long?'
'My fate gave me little choice!'
His mind filled up with the sounds of them
Who had laughed and joked in the past,
They said, 'We knew it would come to this,
But someone had to be last!'

He wandered out in his garden then,
So dark that he couldn't see,
But every one of his friends was there
Hiding behind each tree,
They called and chaffed in the darkness that
Their time had been way back when,
'We're quite content with the lives we led,
Why don't you join us, Ben?'

But Ben sits still in his empty house
While a candle gutters there,
He thinks he'll go when the flame goes out
Sat in his easy chair,
He doesn't think of the future now
For his life was lived in the past,
And his mind is filled with memories
Til the Lord takes him, at last.

Bats in the Belfry

The Church Belfry at Catherine Cross
Was known for its ancient bells,
They'd peal on out before Sunday Mass
And wake the monks in their cells,
The bellringers were a hardy crew
And their timing was superb,
But Joe and John, they didn't get on,
And nor did the Bellman, Herb.

For Herb worked up in the belfry, with
The bells that he thought were his,
He'd tend the stock and the clapper stays
So the clapper wouldn't miss,
He'd set each rope to the ringer's height
To a fraction of an inch,
And woe betide if a ringer died,
Or another called in sick.

He'd call on down to the bellringers,
'Go easy on those ropes,
You wouldn't want to be stretching them,
They're after all, the Pope's!'
But John would glare at his form up there
And call up, between spells,
'Don't interfere with our work down here,
It's we who ring the bells!'

He'd do his best to unsettle Herb
Would leave him in the lurch,
Then try, by ringing the tenor bell
To knock him off his perch,

The bell weighed upwards of three long tons
Would leave John out of breath,
But over time with its endless chime
Herb was going deaf.

Then Herb would leap from the belfry stair
And knock John to the ground,
The bells would ring out of sequence then
And make a terrible sound,
And while they struggled and punched and swore
The villagers would smirk,
'That's Herb and John got a punch-up on,
That Herb is a piece of work!'

So John had gone to the Synod, asked
That the Bellman should be sacked,
'There's nothing he needs to do up there,
I'm sick of being attacked.'
And so the word was carried to Herb
That their need of him was done,
Gave him a week to collect his things
And then, he must be gone.

His final Mass at Catherine Cross
Herb clambered up in the tower,
He'd show them all in his hour of loss
He'd have John in his power,
He loosened the nut that held the bell
To the headstock, up above,
And as it rang with a mighty clang
He gave it a final shove.

Then John strode into the centre, cursing
Looking up at the bell,

But what he saw would forever haunt him
Like some scene from Hell,
The bell was hurtling down towards him
Herb astride the crown,
His eyes a-gleam with revenge, it seemed
As the mighty bell came down.

Herb is buried at Catherine Cross
Not far from the place he fell,
While John was trapped for three long days
Under the dome of the bell,
It took the arm of a crane to lift
And set John free from his pain,
But from then on it was 'Crazy John'
For he clambered out insane!

You Can't Come In!

'If only we could go back,' he said,
'To dot all the 'i's and 'j's,
I'd certainly have a Captain Cook
Again, at my wayward ways.
You must admit that it started well,
There was lots of love to begin.'
She said her piece through a crack in the door,
'There was, but you can't come in!'

'But surely there's time to talk it out,
We've been together so long?'
'You said you'd talk, but you'd only shout,
The things that you did were wrong!'
He slumped against the post of the door
And thought of the things he'd said,
'If only you'd let me in once more,
Without your love, I'm dead!'

'There hasn't been love for many a year,
That flew when you made your choice,
You said, "I'll be working late, my dear,"
When really, you went with Joyce.
You treated me like a perfect fool
When you came in late in the gloom,
And crawled in bed with your back to me,
I could smell her sweet perfume.'

'She never meant anything then to me,
She doesn't mean anything now!'
'That may be true, but I'm telling you
That marked the end of my vow.

I should have cut you adrift before
But I had nowhere to go,
So now, you'd better go find your whore
Or sleep outside in the snow.'

'How could you be so cold and hard
With all that long in the past?'
'I've taken a look at that self-same book
And found me some love at last!'
She stepped aside from the open door
And he thought she'd given in,
But a man stood solid, blocking his way
And he said, 'You can't come in!'

Drama Queen

She sat at the edge of the second floor,
'I'm going to jump!' she cried,
He stood well back from the balcony,
'You lied,' she said, 'you lied!
You swore we'd marry before the Spring
That I'd always be with you…'
'I didn't promise you anything,
It's not what I want to do!'

'Well, why did you lead me on,' she said,
'Did you want to break my heart,
I'll fling myself from this building if
We're going to be apart.'
'I've got a lot of living to do
Before I take a wife,
You said that you'd never tie me down
That you wanted to live your life.'

'I wanted to live my life with you
Is all that I really meant,
But now you're twisting my words, you want
To set up an argument.'
He said, 'You're getting hysterical,
I think that you ought to jump,'
Took one step back, and lifted his foot,
Then planted it in her rump.

She flew off the top of the doll's house
And sat squat on the gravel drive,
Just as her mother motored up,
'I see that you're still alive!'

His father wandered from out the door
And waved to her mother, Gwen,
'I thought I could trust you two out here,
I see what you're doing, Ben!'

'I think she's been watching the Soaps again,
She's always the drama queen,
What have you said to Ben,' said Gwen,
'He's just as bad,' said Deane.
'What have you got to say for yourself,
Apologise to Gwen!'
'She said that she wanted to marry me,
But she knows that I'm only ten!'

The Village That Wasn't There!

I went to stay with an old schoolmate
In the village of Rushing Brooke,
I thought there wouldn't be much to do
So I took a favourite book,
He said he'd only been there a while
For the cottage rent was cheap,
He'd needed to get away, he said,
But never could get to sleep.

His face was haggard, his eyes bloodshot
His hands would tremble and shake,
He said it was close to a fortnight since
He'd started to lie awake,
'I get to the point I'm drifting off
When I hear that terrible knell,
A long slow tolling invades my sleep
From the church that has no bell.'

We sat up talking 'til one o'clock
Then I made my way to bed,
But nothing invaded my sleep that night,
'It won't at first,' he said.
'There's something wanders the street outside
In the hours before the dawn,
Clad in a cowl, or a hooded cloak
But it's gone before the morn.'

From all that I saw of Rushing Brooke
The cottages were quaint,
They certainly had a timeless look,
Could do with a coat of paint.

The roads were rough with a pebbled look
But I saw no folk about,
I passed the Smithy and Fodder store
But the Blacksmith, he was out.

We walked on over to see the church
That was grim, and overgrown,
There'd not been a single service there
Since the Roundheads stormed the town,
But weeds grew up in the vestry, there
Were signs of an ancient fire,
And looking up we could see a space
Right under the old church spire.

'That was the space they hung the bell
But the bell has long been gone,
The Roundheads carried it off, they say,
So it couldn't toll for Rome.
The bell had tolled for the death of Charles
As his head fell under the axe,
The soldiers came for revenge in force
In one of their brute attacks.'

I kept him company every night
But I had to get some sleep,
For days I'd wake and I'd find him still
Awake in a crumpled heap.
I woke one time and I saw him stare
Through the window, into the night,
For there was a ghostly cloak and cowl,
It gave me a sudden fright.

And that's when I heard the tolling bell
For the first time, that he'd said,

The bell from the church, that wasn't there
Was tolling in my head,
I lay awake 'til the sun came up,
Went out to greet the day,
But there the village had tumbled down,
Had long since gone away.

Only the marks of ancient roads,
Foundations that had stood,
There wasn't a cottage left out there
Just an encroaching wood,
The church was standing among the trees
And our cottage, cracked and scarred,
Half of the roof was missing, and
The chimney lay in the yard.

We hurried away to the nearest town
And found an old-style Inn,
My friend had fallen asleep within
A moment of checking in,
He slept and he slept for two whole days
While I asked about the town,
'What of the village of Rushing Brooke?'
But all that they did was frown.

The wife of the keeper of the Inn
Was tidying my room,
I asked her the same old question as
She worked there in the gloom,
'I wouldn't go near to Rushing Brooke
Not now, for a thousand pound,
That's where the soldiers stole the bell
And mowed the villagers down.'

'They say as the place is haunted by
The figure of a monk,
They burnt him alive inside the church
As he tolled the bell by the font.
He lived in a little cottage there,
The only one that stands,
I've heard some tell that they've heard the bell
And seen him, walk in the grounds.'

The Face in the Passing Train

He'd always thought there was somebody
Who could make his life complete,
Among all the faceless people that
He passed in the city street,
But not one ever attracted him
For the faces there were blank,
Lost in their daily routine, at the Mall
And the City Bank.

A city is full of strangers with
No time to smile or greet,
They come in out of the suburbs, and
They jostle, but never meet,
Their lives are hidden from everyone
If they even have a life,
'The girls are married to drones,' he thought,
'And the men to a restless wife.'

'And mine is just as monotonous,'
He thought, as he caught the train,
Hurrying through the sliding doors,
Each morning was just the same.
He caught a glimpse of the human tide
On each station they passed by,
He caught the only Express each day
And that was the reason why.

It hurried away past Ovingham,
It slowed but it didn't stop,
It passed the station at Orly Rue
Raced past the folk at Klop,

It slowed right down to a walking pace
As it sauntered past Beauclaire,
And as it did, his eyes had lit
On a girl that was standing there.

It must have been only seconds that
He could focus on her face,
Her eyes a dazzling blue, her stare
Was arch, but full of grace.
He turned his head as he went on by,
And could swear she stared right back,
Prompting his heart to leap so high
It was like a heart attack.

But the train went on and the girl was gone
As he mopped his fevered brow,
His head said she was the only one
But to find her, it screamed, 'How?'
He took some days off work, and haunted
The station at Beauclaire,
If ever he was to find her, then
He'd surely find her there!

The days went by, but she didn't show
And he thought she'd gone for good,
How would he ever find her again
In this massive neighbourhood?
He watched as his own Express went by
In a burst of springtime rain,
And there was her face at the window,
The face in the passing train.

The Tide is Coming In!

He sat on top of the headland in
The driving, pouring rain,
The way that the clouds were gathering,
He'd never be dry again,
He thought of the girl at Windy Tor
Who had screamed at his only sin,
'You'd better beware of that witch's stare
For the tide is coming in!'

And down in the river valley, there
Was a cottage, made of stones,
Where a temptress with a gleam in her eye
Was juggling spells and bones,
She called the lightning out of the sky
With a book full of ancient tricks,
And blasted the heath round Windy Tor
While lighting her candlesticks.

But up at the Tor, Myfanwy raged
And bubbled and boiled the sea,
She churned it into a raging storm
That her lover could plainly see,
He thought of warning the temptress who
Had entered his eyes and ears,
But heard instead his Myfanwy say,
'It only will end in tears.'

He couldn't go down to the valley, and
He couldn't go up to the Tor,
He could feel his life unravelling
From the bliss that he'd felt before,

A wind soughed up from the valley floor
Full of tempting overtones,
But from the Tor there was something more
An ache, and a Wake of moans.

The sun went down and he turned to go,
He made his way in the dark,
The spell that he was enchanted with
Had finally made its mark,
He turned his back on the love he'd lost,
Went down to the valley floor,
But all he could hear when he got quite near
Was the sea that beat on the shore.

The sea rose up and it poured right in
As it flooded over the plain,
The tide had entered the valley, it
Would never be dry again,
And under the flood of Myfanwy's mood
Was the cottage, made of stones,
While all that was left of the temptress was
A gaggle of spells and bones.

Myfanwy's still up at Windy Tor
And nurses a constant ache,
While his regret hasn't left him yet
For his foolish, one mistake,
He'd sought a spell that she'd love him well
Then fell to a mortal sin,
And always he heard Myfanwy's words,
'The tide is coming in!'

The Homecoming

He'd been away with the army then
For almost twenty years,
And walking back to his village he
Had expected smiles and tears,
He thought his wife would be waiting there
Though his son, he knew, was grown,
He'd been away and protecting them
Though the soldier, now, was home.

He saw the village had barely changed
Though the people stood and stared,
He thought that they were in awe of him
Could it be the village cared?
They took in his battered breastplate and
The dents that marked his greaves,
The helmet that had been battered and
The blood on his chain-mail sleeves.

He'd walked for several miles since when
His horse had collapsed and died,
It weathered many a battle but
Fell foul of the countryside,
But soon he'd take off his armour when
He would meet again his bride,
And she would make him a pottage, and
Rejoice that he hadn't died.

He'd tramped in the lands of Burgundy
He'd fought in the land of Gaul,
He'd taken the Cross to Saladin
And wept at the Wailing Wall.

His face bore scars from the sword and lance
And a mace had raked his back,
From a knight behind who had been struck blind
In a frontal, forced attack.

He'd waded deep in a sea of blood,
He'd trampled a field of bones,
And helped to bury his comrades there
Marking the place with stones,
But now his body was tired and worn
It was leave the field, or die,
His horse had brought him wandering home
To the village of Burton Rye.

His wife came out from the cottage door
And she blanched, and shook in fear,
'I don't know where you are coming from
But you don't belong in here!'
He glanced at the short and thickened form
That he didn't recognise,
'Are you the wife I've been fighting for,
If so, my memory lies!'

'You went away in another life
Leaving none to warm my bed,
I took a shine to the blacksmith here,
Fell in love with him, instead.
It's twenty years since you went away
Did you think you could return?
You've lived the life of a soldier, all
You do, is pillage and burn.'

'I had to go to protect you here,
Out there, it's a world at war,

I've fought the enemy everywhere
To keep the pain from your door.
I loved you when you were slim and young
And your eyes were bright with cheer,'
His shoulders slumped and he turned away,
'I see I'm not wanted here!'

A Long, Long Walk by the Lake

These winter days have been cold and grey,
The sun is hidden above,
Much of my life is spent that way
Since I lost my only love,
For the clouds have entered my heart of hearts,
The cold has withered my smile,
Since ever the day she went away,
When I'd been out for a while.

I'd only been gone an hour or two,
Or so I thought at the time,
But when I returned, her clothes were gone,
She even took some of mine.
The house was empty and cold within
With cobwebs lining each room,
And dust had covered the furniture,
It smelt as rank as a tomb.

The phone had been disconnected, and
The power was off at the wall,
I had to fling open the windows
For any fresh air at all.
The weeds in the lawn were three feet high
Like a jungle, out in the yard,
The cat lay dead in the garden shed,
The tyres were flat on the car.

I called around to her mother's place
To see where she might have been,
Her mother slammed the door in my face
And shouted something obscene.

I panicked then, and I went to see
Where she worked, at Kilroy Square,
But they had a new receptionist,
'She hasn't worked here for a year!'

I bought a paper and saw the date,
And at first it looked all right,
It said the 2nd of August, but
The year then gave me a fright.
It was one year on from the date I left
To walk on down by the lake,
I said to the man behind the stand:
'That year must be a mistake!'

I'd lost a year, and I don't know where,
The sweat stood out on my brow,
Where had I been in the in-between?
I don't know, even now.
I went to wander, down by the lake
Where I'd wandered the year before,
And there was Jane, with a look of pain
On a bench by the lakeside shore.

At first, she'd not even look at me,
She wouldn't answer my plea,
I said, 'Thank God that I've found you, Jane,
Surely you know, it's me!'
She said, 'I've nothing to say to you,
But maybe you'll tell me, Why?
You said that you'd not be gone for long,
You'd not even said Goodbye!'

'I only went for an hour,' I said,
'An hour, or maybe two,

I didn't roam, but I came straight home
And went out looking for you!
I couldn't believe a year had gone,
I must have been going mad!'
She turned, with a scornful look at me,
'As it all turned out, I'm glad.'

She showed me the tiny diamond ring
She wore on her wedding hand,
'I've been engaged for a month, to Gage,
I think he's a better man.'
These winter days have been cold and grey,
The sun is hidden above,
Much of my life is spent that way
Since I lost my only love!

Stranger on the Beach

'I like to wander along the beach,
Meander close to the sea,
To hear the whispering eddies speak,
Refreshing each memory.
When she danced forever along the sand
And she twirled her skirt out wide,
Those were the days that were dear to me
Before the passion died.'

'For way, way back when our world was young
In the distant days of youth,
We'd laugh and play in the surf by day
And at night, we'd search for the truth.
We'd search for the truth beneath the stars
As we lay on our backs to cry,
Her tears had mingled with mine, as soon
As the Moon rose up in the sky.'

'"Why couldn't it always be like this,' she said
And I thought it might,
'The world is turning too soon for us,
And soon may put out the light.'
So we clung together against a world
That would try to tear us apart,
Not knowing time was the enemy
That would age, and harden the heart.'

'Then days would follow each day before,
And weeks would pass like the rain,
That fell unwanted in every life
Since the days of the brother, Cain,

And slowly love would unravel, we
Were telling each other lies,
We tried to avert the other's hurt
But the truth lay deep in our eyes.'

He turned to wander along the beach
Alone, with a grim intent,
His youth was scattering like the leaves
Of the storm-tossed trees that bent,
But dancing on and behind him was
The wraith of the girl that lied,
Shedding tears for the long lost years
As she twirled her skirt out wide.

Frosty Hollow

Down in the depths of Frosty Hollow
The Dell where nobody sleeps,
The eyes are watching one another
In case some human peeps,
It sits in a time of hither and slime
Each side of a distant flood,
Where nothing is really worth the bother,
The ancient Wizard stood.

He stood by the spell of them-and-us
That he spun in a past go round,
That sought the well of the what-they-were
When the skies were close to the ground,
And nobody sought to leave the Hollow
Except in a cowl or hood,
The ways of men were hard to swallow
Outside the enchanted wood.

The stars that sparkled up in the trees
Had promised a cold come in,
But the Wizard ruled the things that matter
And various types of sin,
He ruled the currents that gave them breath,
And told of the marsh outside,
Where those who left met an evil death
In the end, so nobody tried.

And slowly, he would increase the size
Of the Dell to the world outside,
The Dell would spread on the bones of the dead
He said, in his sin of pride,

But the eyes were fed with suspicions, and
They looked to each other first,
And the first in Hell were those in the Dell
Who looked at the Wizard and cursed.

Down in the depths of Frosty Hollow
The Dell where nobody sleeps,
The eyes are watching one another
In case some human peeps,
It sits in a time of hither and slime
Each side of a distant flood,
And there you'll find an ancient Wizard
Who lies in a pool of blood.

The Fifty Dollar Ride

We were way up there on the Ferris Wheel
When it came to a sudden stop,
We'd only got on for the final ride
And it left us up at the top.
'What are they doing?' said Imogen,
As we first began to doubt,
Then looking down to the distant ground
The lights of the Fair went out.

'Surely they know that we're still up here!'
There was panic in her voice,
I tried to bellow, and then to shout,
They had left us little choice.
The lights of the cars had streamed below
With the last ones, headed away,
The wind up there put a chill in the air
And the Wheel began to sway.

'I think I'm going to be sick,' she cried,
And I said, 'Please, not on me!'
I wrapped her up in my coat and tried
To calm her misery.
'It's always the same with you,' she said,
'But it keeps on getting worse,
The moment we're down, and on the ground
I'm going to get a divorce.'

We'd only gone on the Ferris Wheel
For a place to talk things out,
I wanted to get her away from home
To a place where she couldn't shout.

She'd sworn she'd never divorce me that
She'd make life living hell,
I had to make her want a divorce
As much as me, as well.

'So I get blamed for the Ferris Wheel,
Did I tell the guy to stop?
How could I know he'd forget us here
And leave us perched at the top?'
'It always happens, you wired the stove
So the whole damn thing was live,
Then I got thrown when I switched it on,
It's lucky I'm still alive.'

'Then out in the boat, we nearly sank
When you put the boat in a spin,
It filled with water when you forgot
To put the drain plug in.'
'I know, I know, I'm a jinx,' I said,
It always happens to me,
Perhaps you'd better get a divorce
Then you'll be finally free.'

We didn't speak for a solid hour,
Sat as far apart as we could,
And then I lit up a cigarette
To dispel my cold, black mood.
Our marriage had really hit the pits,
It was never going to do,
I'd not been happy since Imogen
Had turned to a carping shrew.

I'd never done anything right for her,
And never could make amends,

She always tried to humiliate me
By telling all of her friends.
She said I was good for nothing, but
To give her my weekly cheque,
At times I barely restrained myself
From seizing her round the neck.

An hour went by, and the Wheel began
To take us down to the ground,
Someone had seen my cigarette
It seemed, said the man from town.
She shrieked and screamed as she stalked away
At the guy that I knew as Nick,
As I slipped him his fifty bucks, and said:
'It seems to have done the trick!'

Bed of Roses

If life was a bed of roses, then
My neighbour would fit the bill,
He'd built him a twelve room mansion
Next to me, on top of the hill,
It made my cottage look down at heel
Til I grew a hawthorn hedge,
So nobody could look down on me
Though he did, from up on a ledge.

His name was Jeremy Harmon, and
His wife was Amanda Cale,
I'd played with him in the schoolyard, though
He'd won him a place at Yale,
He'd spent his life in America
Though he'd come back home to wed,
And stole the only woman I loved
From our own pre-bridal bed.

She'd fallen hard for his Ivy League
And his Yves St. Laurent suits,
His rented Aston Martin, and
His R.M. Williams boots.
He'd made a pile and he flaunted it
Before heading back to the States,
Taking Amanda Cale with him,
I got her note too late.

'I'm sorry John, and I know it's wrong
But he swept me off my feet,
We're going to live in Chicago, where
He said that life's a treat.

We'll live in a condominium
And he promised me a maid,
Oh don't be sad, for I'm rather glad,
Just think of the love we made.'

And that was the last I heard of them
For almost twenty years,
The name of Jeremy Harmon passed
My lips, as a sort of curse,
I just got on with my life, but brought
No woman to my bed,
My head was full of Amanda Cale
And her betrayal, instead.

They turned up totally unexpected,
Rang my front doorbell,
'We're going to be your neighbour, Hey!
It's good to see you, pal.'
He seemed to be totally unaware
Of the grief he'd caused, back when,
I held my tongue and I kept my peace,
'Okay, I'll see you then.'

A year went by and the house went up
And I grew my hawthorn hedge,
Amanda worked in the garden planting
Seeds and lawn and sedge,
I did my best to avoid her, though
She tried to keep things light,
But chuckled things like, 'Remember when…'
And I'd say, 'That's not right!'

'You made your bed when you left with him,
There are no memories,

I saw you last in his Aston Martin
Waving through the trees.'
'That was a mistake, I know,' she said,
'But things could turn out right,
He goes away on his business trips
And I'm all alone at night.'

I'm sure I said that it wasn't on,
I'm sure I told her to go,
But she was given to plots and schemes
About things I didn't know.
She asked me once for a bag of lime
To use on her roses bed,
And like a fool, I gave her the tool
To let her back in my bed.

Jeremy went on a business trip
And didn't come home at all,
She said he'd gone to America,
Their marriage had gone to the wall.
She came to cry on my shoulder then
Each day, for almost a year,
And in the end, I had given in,
She seemed in a deep despair.

Her garden then was magnificent
For her roses were in bloom,
'I've never seen such a great display,'
I said, one afternoon.
'You can thank my husband, Jeremy,
He's been working, all this time,
You're tied to me for eternity
For you supplied the lime!'

Return to the Light that Failed

The night was dark, in a brooding pall
With thunderheads at its core,
But only the sound of heaving swells
Were heard to break on the shore.
The headland dark where the Lighthouse stood
With not a glimmer of light,
It hadn't been lit for a hundred years
But a beam would stream that night.

The sea was grumbling in its deeps
Cast heaps of weed on the sand,
Much like a drunken Cornishman
Disgorging his contraband,
The swell, built up as the squalls came in
Made the sea erupt from its depths,
Casting an age old Barquentine
Up high, on an angry crest.

Shook free from its hundred year old bed
Untangled from miles of weed,
The Barquentine with its forty dead
Had finally now been freed,
A flag that carried the fleur-de-lis
Hung limply down from the mast,
And tangled up in the rigging was
The body of Captain Jacques.

An aura shone round the Barquentine
In a pale, blue ghostly light,
Caught in a time warp, in-between
They rose as a man that night.

They gathered up on the rotting deck
Each cannon, covered in rust,
And glared at the lighthouse on the hill,
A light that they couldn't trust.

A wraith of a woman, stood that night
By the keeper, looking down,
The face of a woman, creased in fear
As the Barque had come aground,
She had been the wife of Captain Jacques
Had been left ashore, and fled,
Up to the keeper of the light
Where she shared his meagre bed.

'I didn't think he'd be back so soon,'
She'd stood by the light, and cried,
'If he finds us both alone up here
It's better that we had died.'
The keeper held her trembling form
As the storm built up that night,
'I'd never allow him to bring you harm,'
He said, as he struck the light.

The crew looked up at the Lighthouse
And they heard a woman scream,
From up on the headland, deep in fright
As the keeper lit the beam,
And Jacques looked up, and he saw his wife
Lit up by the sudden light,
'My God,' he cried, 'that's Jacqueline,
There was infamy that night!'

The pair looked down as the men had leapt
To shore, with their swords held high,

They'd waited over a hundred years
But knew that their time was nigh.
He'd struck the light when he saw their ship
Head in to threaten his whore,
And watched as the ship had broken up
In Eighteen fifty-four.

There are nights when the light of former wrongs
Returns to visit the shame,
To balance eternal justice for
The centuries, left in pain,
The ghostly sailors dragged them down
To the Barquentine, at last,
And as the sea had reclaimed the ship
They hung them both from the mast.

Lightning Strike!

She worked part-time as a seamstress,
An ordinary sort of girl,
But one with a dash of blue-eyed wit,
An endearing brunette curl.
I'd plucked up the courage to ask her out,
For me it was more than like,
And everything seemed to be going well
Before the lightning strike.

One day we walked to the countryside
By the fields of wheat and hay,
Rambling on by the hedgerows there
On a darkening Autumn day.
I stole a kiss in a grove of trees
From the lips that taste like wine,
And then she whispered her love for me
All coy, with her eyes a-shine.

The clouds were gathering overhead
And soon it began to rain,
We sought some shelter, under a ledge
Right next to a field of grain,
But she was nervous, clung to my hand
When the thunder growled on high,
'The gods are grumbling over the land,'
She said, and began to cry.

I said, 'There's nothing to fret about,
It's only an Autumn storm,
We'll just stay here and we'll wait it out,'
But Michelle was lost, forlorn.

A mighty clap came from overhead
And she screamed, ran out in the rain,
When a bolt of lightning struck her there,
A flash, then a shriek of pain!

I dashed on out, and I picked her up
But her clothes were burned and charred,
Her hair was white and it stood on end,
Full of some potent charge.
She rolled her eyes and she looked at me
Her face, a panic attack,
And then I saw that her sky-blue eyes
Had turned to a deep jet black.

The clouds were tumbling overhead
Though the rain was passing on,
The lightning strikes were further away
She cried, 'Has the thunder gone?'
She sat there trembling in my arms
But focussed her gaze on high,
And said at last, as she stared above,
'There are demons up in the sky!'

She spent a month in the hospital
And they said she'd be okay,
I'll never forget the way she looked
When I picked her up that day,
She huddled up in the car and said,
'The world outside has changed,
For fire and flashes are everywhere
There's a lightning strike in my brain.'

'And now, in the darkest corners I
Have visions of swarms of rats,

While up in the eaves, and waiting there,
A host of vampire bats,
There's crawling things that I didn't see
Before, when my eyes were blue,
And awful spiders with fourteen legs,
Right now, they're crawling on you.'

I took her home, and put her to bed,
I thought that she needed rest,
A week went by, but she'd sit and cry,
I thought she was quite obsessed.
Then I started hearing crawling things
At night, when I went to sleep,
And woke to a creature on my chest
That made my own flesh creep.

There's demons up in the clouds,' she said,
'And fires scorching the ground,
And everywhere that I look, I see
Where evil spirits abound.'
I couldn't take it a moment more,
These things invaded my mind,
I did what anyone else would do,
And now, Michelle is blind!

The Spyders

I'm not into modern music since
The Spyders came to town,
One of those painted-tainted groups
That you often see around,
But Anne-Marie was younger than me
And she went with every craze,
She called me a boring dinosaur
At the height of those Spyder days.

I've always been a conservative,
I don't get carried away,
I know whatever is going down
It won't be there next day,
The house was full of discarded things
That had lost their first allure,
The moment she saw the Next Big Thing
Come barrelling through the door.

The Spyder thing was over the top
I said to her more than twice,
'They'll be forgotten within a month,'
She replied, 'That wasn't nice!
Why do you always bring me down,
You're turning into a grump!'
So I wasn't allowed to criticise,
She put me under the pump.

She came back home from the hairdresser's
With a bouffant type of style,
Sprayed and lacquered so it was hard,
She slept upright for a while.

She said that it was the Spyder look
That the girls all thought it great,
With hair like a spider's legs each side,
Bobbing around her face.

I shook my head, but I held my tongue
There was nothing to be gained,
For anything that I said just then
Would bring me future pain.
The following day, she went away
And she came back home that night,
With a square of plaster on her neck
And I thought, 'This isn't right!'

She said that she'd got a small tattoo
And I nearly had a fit,
I said, 'That's going to be there for life,'
So she wouldn't show me it.
She kept me waiting a week to see
The blue-black spider there,
Crawling up the nape of her neck
And heading into her hair.

'How shall I ever kiss you there,'
I howled, while shaking my head,
'That's the end of our necking days,'
'Oh don't be soft,' she said.
We barely spoke for a week back then
It was just the early Spring,
She spent her time round the roses with
Her bouffant, and that 'thing'.

There's always a lot of spiders webs
Outside, at that time of year,

And Anne-Marie must have brushed through them
And got them caught in her hair,
For days she said that she wasn't well
That she must have had the flu,
But then one morning I woke in bed
To see that her lips were blue.

Her head fell back on the head rest, and
Disturbed the bouffant style,
And thousands of tiny spiders rushed
On out of her hair, meanwhile,
They swarmed on over her shoulders,
From the nest she had on her head,
But Anne-Marie was beyond it now
For Anne-Marie was dead!

I never listen to music now,
I turn off the radio,
Whenever the Spyder's music's played
On the Old-Time Late Late Show.
The band broke up a decade ago
And the lead is doing time,
He said that his skin began to crawl
With the tatts all down his spine.

The Storyteller

He sat in a small compartment by
The window, on a train,
The passengers huddled around him
Saying, 'Tell that one again!'
He spoke in a low and measured voice
As they held their breath, to stare,
Watching his hands, as they described
Vague circles in the air.

There wasn't a sound outside, except
The carriage, clickety-clack,
A sound that would tend to hypnotise
As the train sped down the track,
In every one of his listeners
Was a picture, in each mind,
That spoke to them of that better life
Which had been too hard to find.

And seagulls circled the skies above
As he primed their minds with 'If…'
And led them all in a straggly line
To stand at the top of a cliff.
The sea was blue and the clouds were grey
And the rocks below sublime,
As they teetered there for a moment where
They stood, at the edge of time.

For then he'd show them a garden, with
The form of an only child,
Who seemed to be so familiar
That most of them there had smiled,

The scent of a pink wisteria
Had wafted the carriage air,
And then their tears rolled back the years
As they whispered, 'I was there!'

He showed them a woman in mourning
With a cape, and a darkened veil,
Who knelt alone by a headstone,
Each listeners face was pale.
The bell of the church began to toll
As it sounded someone's knell,
His face was the face of the gravedigger
As he held them in his spell.

The carriage was filled with waves of fear,
The carriage was filled with joy,
He'd tell of the death of a mountaineer,
Of a child with a much-loved toy,
Their tears they'd dry as the train came in
To the tale of a Scottish Kirk,
And one by one they would rise to leave
And head off the train, to work.

But the Storyteller would stay on board
And close the compartment door,
His restless hands were trembling still
As his eyes stared down at the floor.
The train heads into the future while
The past is deep in his well,
He sits and weeps in the corner for
The tales that he doesn't tell.

Angel Dust

An angel fell to the earth one day
And lay with a broken wing,
I saw her lying out on the path
And thought I was seeing things.
'Are you really what I think you are?'
I said, but I saw she cried,
So picked her gently up in my arms,
'I'd better get you inside.'

Her tears were staining her pale white cheeks,
And weeds were caught in her hair,
The wing was twisted and limp, I saw,
And I couldn't help but stare.
'I think I must look a fright,' she said,
And dabbed away at her tears,
'I flew straight into a plane, and still,
The engines ring in my ears.'

I laid her down on the couch inside
Stood back, was taking her in,
'I thought you couldn't be seen by men,
You've set me to wondering!'
Her dress was white, but was stained with mud
From the place she'd lain, by the gate,
And on the wing was a trace of blood
While feathers fell in the grate.

'We'd best get that in a splint,' I said,
And busied myself a while,
Tearing a sheet into long white strips
And setting the kettle to boil.

'I'd take you down to the hospital
But the shock would be hard to gauge,
They'd probably call in the military,
And lock you up in a cage.'

'I only came to escort you in,'
She said, 'and now all this fuss.
You should have been walking the street by now,
And due to be hit by a bus!
They're going to be mad when I get back home,
I've botched the eternal clock,
And you'll live on past the danger zone,
While I'll end up in the dock.'

An icy shiver ran down my spine
Like someone walked on my grave,
'You say I was going to die today,
But you were late, so I'm saved!'
'If you can see me you're still not safe
Beware of all things on wheels,
They'll have to revise your life spell now
If a few more years appeals.'

'I'll take whatever you've got,' I said,
'I'm not quite ready to go,
There's too many books I haven't read,
And women to, well, you know!'
They must have made a decision then
For the wind blew through in a gust,
Instead of an angel, sitting, there
Was a cloud of Angel Dust.'

The Bull Roarer

We'd travelled more than a hundred miles
From the nearest outback town,
The sun was roasting the plains out there
And the heat was getting us down,
We'd left all the eucalypts behind
And there wasn't a patch of green,
Only a scrubby saltbush there
Where the natives used to dream.

We halted just as the sun went down
And Miranda let out a sigh,
'Have ever you seen such stars as these?'
And pointed up at the sky,
The heavens shone with a mighty glow
From the stars that glittered, proud,
Each was lighting the earth below
From the inky black of its shroud.

But underneath us the ground was hot
And the track it lay, bone dry,
There'd not been even a single drop
Of rain, since the last July,
We huddled up in the four wheel drive
As the air began to chill,
I pulled a blanket across our knees
And we slept for a little while.

Miranda had some Arunta blood
From her great-grandmother's side,
She'd learned of some of their culture, and
She had the Arunta pride,

We woke to a distant whirring sound
And Miranda sat up straight,
And murmured, 'That's a Tjurunga
Trying to open heaven's gate.'

'The white men call it a Bull Roarer,'
She said, with a hint of fear,
'And I'm forbidden to hear it, for
It's not for a woman's ear.
They'll kill me if they should find me here
For breaking their sacred law,'
She slid down over her seat, and sat
Her head down, close to the floor.

I climbed on out of the cab, and stood
Surveying the dark surround,
The whirring seemed to be closer now,
And the pitch went up and down,
An icy chill ran along my spine
As I saw a movement there,
Something slithering over the ground
Not far from where we were.

I froze in shock, and I held my breath
When I saw a pair of eyes,
Both the colour of rubies, and
Of quite enormous size,
And then I saw the head of the snake
As it ploughed a furrow, deep,
Its body the colours of rainbows, then
Miranda took a peep.

She said, 'It's the Rainbow Serpent,'
As the whirring sound went on,

Covered her ears and shut her eyes
And said, 'It'll soon be gone.'
I climbed back into the cab and locked
The door, and lay down flat,
Trembled in fear, I'd never seen
A snake as big as that.

The dawn was gradually breaking as
I took a look outside,
And there, where the ground had been quite flat
Was a creek, ten metres wide,
And water, straight from the Queensland rains
Was pouring over the land,
Sluicing along the new creek bed
Where before, there was only sand.

I'd never believed in the Dreamtime
Or the tales that the natives tell,
But somewhere the Rainbow Serpent roams
With eyes from heaven or hell,
We turned the nose of the jeep around,
Drove back to the town once more,
I'll never return to the desert, where
You can hear the Bull Roarer's roar!

Blood, Red Blood...

The night outside was a solid mist
You couldn't see past three feet,
Or so she thought, the Telephonist
As she came back in from the street.
There was no point following Jill and Tim
For the mist had swallowed them up,
They'd wandered out for a drink before
To head for the 'Stirrup Cup'.

So Caryn finally went inside
And stood by the lounge room door,
There was blood, red blood on the candlestick,
There was blood, red blood on the floor,
She opened her mouth and she tried to scream
But couldn't begin to shout,
She seemed to be locked in a crazy dream
And the folk in the house were out.

There wasn't a body that she could see
But chills ran over her spine,
She wondered about her sister, Jill,
Then thought, 'I'm sure she's fine!'
But Tim, now there was a moody man
And his anger knew no bounds,
She'd hidden from him in her room before
When he'd stomped the house and grounds.

She staggered into the street again
There must be someone to call,
She felt her way through the garden gate
There was blood, red blood on the wall,

And a trail of blood lay under her feet
That led to the 'Stirrup Cup',
She felt the gorge rise up in her throat,
She was close to throwing up.

She felt her way through the evening mist
Stuck close to the kerb as well,
There was blood all over the bailiwick
As she called her sister's cell,
It rang and rang 'til it rang right out
And Caryn let out a moan,
But then a text on her tiny screen
That said one word, 'Alone!'

She felt so faint that she stumbled then
Her head was a pounding wreck,
There was blood, red blood in her auburn hair,
There was blood on her cheek and neck,
She seemed to glide to the further wall
And caught herself looking down,
Down to the blood where her body lay
All crumpled, there on the ground.

And Jill and Tim found her lying there
As they walked by a stranded bus,
'Oh God, it's Caryn, my sister, Tim,
She must have been following us!'
They called the Police and they got back home
To find the blood on the wall,
There was blood, red blood on the candlestick
And blood all over the hall.

While Caryn drifts in a nightly mist
That you can't see past three feet,

She used to be a Telephonist
But now she's lost in the street.
Wherever she turns there's blood, red blood
But she can't believe it's hers,
She seems to be locked in a crazy dream
Of a never ending curse!

Martha's Broom

She lay awake in her tiny bed
And she waited for the dawn,
For then she'd be turning five, they said,
The day that she was born,
She hid her head right under the sheet
And she giggled, now and then,
Thinking about the presents like
They'd given once, to Ben.

For Ben was her older brother and
He'd recently been eight,
Was given a bike, though second-hand,
And Ben had thought it great,
He'd fallen off it a dozen times
And she saw he'd skinned his knees,
But how she would love a bike like his,
She lay and she whispered, 'Please!'

He'd also got lots of lollipops
And he wouldn't even share,
The one that she stole got sticky, and
Got tangled up in her hair,
But best of all was the parcel that
Unwrapped, was a railway train,

It puffed real steam and its livery gleamed
Til he left it out in the rain.

The sun peeped over the window-sill
And she thought she'd take a look,
For lying there on her counterpane
Was a well-thumbed Cookery Book,
And dimly, stood in the corner of
Her sparsely furnished room,
Was a brush and pan and a black lead can
And a new, short-handled broom.

'You're old enough for the chores,' she heard
As her mother watched her sob,
'You can start by filling the kettle,
Then you can place it on the hob,
You'll use the pan for the ashes that
You'll be scraping from the grate,
Then spread them out by the roses, on
The ones by the garden gate.'

'You'll sweep the floors in the morning with
That nice new broom you got,
Attend to all of the blacking when
The oven's not so hot,
And then you'll help with the cooking, so
You'll come home straight from school,
Your Da' has need of his supper, so
You'll work, not play the fool.'

The broom had come from a gypsy van
That was camped out on the green,
Was shaped and whittled by gypsy men
To whisk the meadow clean,

It carried with it a gypsy spell
That was woven in a hearse,
To whisk it well, or a taste of hell,
Along with a gypsy curse.

When Martha picked up the broom she felt
The power spread in her hands,
She whisked away to a gypsy tune
She'd heard from the caravans,
She whisked the ashes over the floor,
Put blacking over her nose,
Spilled the kettle over the hob
And ruined her father's clothes.

Her mother started to beat the girl
But the broom then beat her back,
Whisking her out through the open door
And putting her under attack,
It swept the porch right into a heap
It piled the boards of the floor,
Tearing them up from the joists, and then
Sweeping them out the door.

It whisked the lid off the blacking can
And spread black over the walls,
Til Martha's mother ran down the street
To the sound of squeals and squalls,
So Martha's father bought her a doll
That could do all kinds of tricks,
While Martha waved the broom at her Ma,
'Just wait til I am six!'

Crossword

I was doing a crossword puzzle
Yesterday, to pass the time,
The clues were all about animals
Both across, and down the line,
The wife was out in the kitchen
And I'd call the harder clues,
While she'd reply with a patient sigh
As she cooked two different stews.

It wasn't as easy as I'd thought
Some clues were quite obscure,
Though each would bring up some animal
That we should have known, for sure,
But as I scribbled across the squares
I found some didn't fit,
I'd call, 'Lynette, have you worked it yet?'
But she'd never heard of it.

She'd said, 'Two heads are better than one,'
And I thought she might be right,
The names that came out too long, I thought
Must be an oversight,
But when they clashed with the downward clues
And I crumpled up my hat,
That furry purr by the fireside there
Was just a common Dat.

And things that flew in the night became
Some thing they called a Rel,
They must be horrible creatures, like
Some creature based in Hell,

But as it crossed the Ordothlicon
I knew it must be right,
For on the left was a Rerr that leapt
On a dark and stormy night.

She said that really my spelling might
Be not quite up to scratch,
The ones that I knew as Pidgins flew
The coop in quite a batch,
And honey gathering Lees in trees
Were paired with wild Gorrils,
While Madgers seemed to be burrowing
All though the distant hills.

'I've never heard of these animals,'
I said, in quite a stew,
Lynette called out from the kitchen that
She didn't know them, too,
I walked around and I locked the doors
And I set each window latch,
In case that some of them wandered in
Like Carroll's Bandersnatch.

I'm loth to wander the streets at night
If Rogs are on the prowl,
And keep away from the Cagpies nests
And the things that say 'Miaowl',
It seems that Berons are on the beach
And Peagulls in the air,
Lynette said better we stay inside
Than to get Peegull in our hair.

Cliffhanger

He pondered over the note he wrote,
Sat hunched and cold in his chair,
He nodded once as he read it then
And signed the bottom with flair,
The house was not even stirring then
As he rose, looked out at the sea,
It said, 'By the time you see this, Jen,
I'll be hanging from some old tree.'

Then he slipped on out to the breaking day
As the dawn was beginning to spread,
He should have been further along than this,
By now, he should have been dead.
He'd heard them stir in the attic room
When he'd come in late from the bay,
His wife and a lifelong friend of his
Who'd thought he was still away.

He'd heard the sound of them making love
As he crept to the attic door,
His face turned white in the passage light
As he sank to the passage floor.
The tears had welled at his eyes at last
As he crept back down the stairs,
He'd lost a friend and his woman, Jen,
And the love that he thought was theirs.

He wandered over the grassland there
To the woods at the edge of the cliff,
But not forgetting to take the coil
Of rope, he held at his hip.

He wondered how many times they'd met
While he was away at sea,
And laughed, the minute his back was turned
To leave him no dignity.

Then pictures rose in his troubled mind
That he shouldn't have had to think,
He cursed himself, for he must be blind
When his friend had tipped her a wink,
The pain was really too much to bear
For he'd lost not one, but two,
He'd loved them both, she'd broken her oath
And his friend had betrayed him too.

He found a tree, hung over the cliff
That was old and gnarled and bent,
With a sturdy branch that would do the trick,
It was too late to relent.
He flung the rope and he made it fast
Then fashioned the hangman's knot,
It would swing him out and over the sea
And send him where time forgot.

He tugged on the rope to test the branch
To see if it took his weight,
Dropped the loop down over his head
When a voice cried out, 'Just wait!'
He turned to see his Jen on the path
That ran alongside the cliff,
'What are you doing, my love, my love,
Is my love worth less than this?'

She said she'd gone for a walk that night,
Hadn't been able to sleep,

'Your friend is up in the attic room
With a woman from Warley Heath.
He only met her a week ago,'
She said, 'and borrowed the bed.
He said that you wouldn't mind, but I
Wasn't impressed,' she said.

He pulled the rope from over his head
And he hugged his woman tight,
'I'm such a fool, but I thought that you
And he… It was such a fright!'
The sun beamed down and it seemed to say
That a love so strong was rare,
While a gnarled old tree drooped over the sea
With its rope, still hanging there.

The Butcher's Hook

The body lay in a mound of hay
That was all piled up by the forge,
He took one look at the butcher's hook
And the sick rose up in his gorge,
He peered on down at the bloodied face
There was nothing that could be done,
But held his breath when he saw that death
Had taken the blacksmith's son.

He looked around for a sign of life
But the shop and the forge were cold,
The blacksmith Kirk hadn't come to work
Though he'd seen him, out in the fold,
And darling Kate would be calling in,
His fate whirled round in his head,
What would she think when she found him there
With the love of her life stone dead?

The villagers knew no love was lost,
They'd fought at the village fete,
All over the hand of the pretty one,
The hand of their darling Kate,
But George was on an apprenticeship
For his father had owned the forge,
While Faber was a farm labourer,
So Kate had gone off with George.

But now George lay in a pile of hay
And he wouldn't be dating Kate,
So Faber thought that he shouldn't stay
Though he'd left it a little late.

He didn't know if they'd seen him come,
He couldn't be seen to go,
They'd think that he was the only one
To deliver the killer blow.

He heard a rustle within the store
And the sweat broke out on his head,
He knew if somebody found him there
That he'd be better off dead.
He peered silently through the door
And into the corner gloom,
And Kate was sobbing, there on the floor
In the darkest part of the room.

Her bouffant hair was a tangled mess
Her dress was tattered and frayed,
It didn't take but a single guess
To see the part that she'd played,
For blood was mingling with her tears
Her bodice was stained deep red,
'He stole my innocence,' she exclaimed,
'I hit him just once,' she said.

Now Faber sits in a darkened cell
To wait for the hangman's rope,
The Judge had asked, but he wouldn't tell
So now he's bereft of hope.
He'd told the court that he'd stumbled in
On the blacksmith's son, and rape,
And hit him once with a butcher's hook
For the sake of the darling Kate.

But Kate was strolling with someone new
On the day that they pinned his hands,

And led him up to the gallows floor
To pay for the court's demands,
She never gave him a thought that day
Though the blacksmith thought he knew,
And lay in wait with a butcher's hook
As Kate was passing through.

Index of First Lines

An angel fell to the earth one day	160
An Isle rose up from the ocean swell	108
Down in the depths of Frosty Hollow	141
Driving blind through a flurry of mist	103
Garth lay still in the gilded cage	73
Giselle went down to the Supermart	32
He came on home to an empty house	35
He'd always thought there was somebody	129
He'd been away with the army then	133
He pondered over the note he wrote	172
He sat in a small compartment by	158
He sat on top of the headland in	131
He stood at the back, and looked around	116
He was sat in a quaint old country pub	98
I'd come back home from an early shift	78
I'd driven a bus for thirty years	53
I'd known Dionne since her coming out	88
I'd see strange lights in the garden shed	57
If life was a bed of roses, then	146
I followed her over the countryside	92
If only we could go back,' he said,	121
I like to wander along the beach	139
I'm not into modern music since	155
I pass my time with the living dead	96
I sat up late with a Shoot-em-up	94
It looked all right through the windows of	15
It was after the funeral service	70
It was just on the stroke of midnight	12
I was doing a crossword puzzle	170
I was part of the crew of a Sloop-of-War	20
I went to stay with an old schoolmate	125

My first wife went with a guy called Bob	41
My uncle lived in a big old house	7
Samantha worked in the Take-away	84
She'd lived alone since her husband left	100
She'd walk on out to the balcony	48
She lay awake in her tiny bed	167
She sat at the edge of the second floor	123
She wandered down to the rocky beach	29
She was always a bit of an actress	51
She worked part-time as a seamstress	152
The body lay in a mound of hay	175
The Church Belfry at Catherine Cross	118
The ground had rumbled for quite some time	10
The hills were awash with winter rain	60
The house had an evil aspect as	23
The Inn he kept at the crossroads shone	66
The Little Withering Rep. had met	26
The night outside was a solid mist	165
The night was dark, in a brooding pall	149
There are some who consider suicide	18
There's a glow in the sky this morning	69
There's a scurrying sound of something,	30
There wasn't much left of the woods out	44
These winter days have been cold and grey	136
The Whispering Wall of Shah La Mere	114
The wind was swaying the treetops as	75
They'd gone to live in an old stone house	37
They say she suffered from visions, so	81
We'd bought a cottage, but sight unseen	62
We'd travelled more than a hundred miles	162
We were friends of a sort, when we were	111
We were way up there on the Ferris Wheel	143

www.ingramcontent.com/pod-product-compliance
Lightning Source LLC
Chambersburg PA
CBHW061647040426
42446CB00010B/1625